*WAR PLANES OF THE FIRST WORLD WAR*

# FIGHTERS

## VOLUME TWO

## GREAT BRITAIN

## J. M. BRUCE
M.A., F.R.Hist.S., A.R.Ae.S.

**MACDONALD : LONDON**

SBN 356 01473 8

*First published in 1968 by*
*Macdonald & Co. (Publishers) Ltd.*
*49 Poland Street, London W.1*
*Made and Printed in Great Britain by*
*Purnell & Sons, Ltd.*
*Paulton (Somerset) and London*

# INTRODUCTION

The first volume in this series contained compact histories of British fighting aircraft of the 1914–18 war from the A.D. Scout to the Port Victoria P.V.8. This book continues, in alphabetical sequence of manufacturers' names, from the Robey single-seat scouts to the Sopwith 2F.1 Camel.

It was originally intended that this second volume should deal with all the British fighters not recorded in Volume I, but so much significant material came to light that overcompression of the fascinating histories of many Royal Aircraft Factory, Sopwith and Vickers types would have produced an inadequate document. The publishers therefore agreed, generously and sensibly, that the right course to follow was to spread the remaining British fighters over two further volumes. Thus Volume III will contain the histories of aircraft from the Sopwith Hippo to the Wight quadruplane.

In this volume the histories of such aircraft as the B.E.12, F.E.2a, S.E.2 and Sopwith 2F.1 are somewhat different from those that have been generally accepted heretofore, and reflect the results and interpretation of recent research and discoveries.

Pictorially, some aircraft are here portrayed for the first time, in a few cases by photographs that may not be of the highest quality but are presented without apology because they are of unusual interest.

For the general-arrangement drawings I am indebted to Michael Badrocke, Don Clayton, Hugh Cowin, Peter Griffin, John Marsden and Derek Tattersall. My admiration of their skill is matched only by my appreciation of the patience they have displayed in the face of my briefings and comments. Thanks to their efforts it can again be said that sound three-view drawings of many of the aircraft herein described are presented for the first time. And into the histories are built the contributions, some of them substantial, of friends who have helped me similarly in the past. The massive and continuing aid freely given over many years by Stuart Leslie is again one of the cornerstones of this book; and to Wing Commander N. H. F. Unwin, M.B.E., R.A.F. (ret'd), I am especially indebted for his great help in many matters relating to the Royal Aircraft Factory aeroplanes. Frank Cheesman, Ken Molson, Bruce Robertson, Ann Tilbury of *Flight International*, and Frank Smith (who was Librarian of the Royal Aeronautical Society while this volume was in preparation) and his staff have all given generous assistance that I acknowledge gratefully.

J. M. BRUCE

# ROBEY-PETERS SCOUTS

On the outbreak of war the Air Department of the Admiralty pursued a vigorous policy of expanding aircraft production by giving to firms without experience or early intention of building aircraft contracts for the manufacture under licence of aeroplanes and seaplanes designed by some of the firms that made up the tiny aircraft industry of the time. One such firm was the engineering concern of Robey & Co. Ltd., of Lincoln.

Their first products were the Sunbeam-powered Sopwith Gun Bus and the Short 184 seaplane. Robey & Co. became major contractors for the Short, and also built small batches of Henri Farman F.27s and Maurice Farman Longhorns for the Admiralty.

The firm set up a design department of their own in 1915 with Mr. J. A. Peters as their chief designer. No adequate record of his early designs appears to have survived, but there is no doubt that two of these were intended to be single-seat scouts. It seems that both were designed in 1915, but it is unknown which came first.

Although the airframe of the Robey tractor scout was built, it seems that no engine was ever fitted, but it is believed that the intended power unit was the 80-h.p. Clerget. The aircraft was a simple, single-bay biplane, conventional in every way and apparently inspired by the successful Sopwith Tabloid. Ailerons were fitted to upper and lower wings and were actuated by wheel control; the small balanced rudder resembled that of the Tabloid.

*The uncovered airframe of the Robey-Peters tractor scout.*

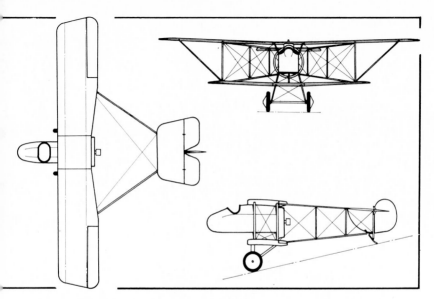

It has been said that the Robey tractor scout was sent to Brooklands, but the reason for doing so has yet to be discovered. No record of its fate seems to have survived, but its abandonment has been attributed to the fact that its tail surfaces were too small. It seems more likely that it was realised that the Robey could not hope to compete with other contemporary types of scout.

Satisfactory proof of the completion of the Robey pusher scout has yet to be found. According to one source the aircraft was built but crashed on its first flight. However, this was precisely the fate of the later three-seat Davis-gun carrier, consequently it is difficult to be certain that the report relates to the pusher scout. Of all the Robey designs it is the one for which the most complete data have survived, but this is probably fortuitous, and the figures for weights and performance may be no more than estimates.

It was a compact biplane with wings of unequal span, the extensions of the upper wing being strut-braced. The nacelle was midway between the wings and was connected by struts to both upper and lower centre sections; the surviving drawings depict a fairing between the top of the nacelle and the upper centre section. The pilot would have had an excellent outlook in all directions vital in combat.

The Robey pusher scout was designed for two alternative power units: the 80-h.p. Gnome rotary or the 90-h.p. Salmson M.7 water-cooled radial. The estimated top speeds with these engines were, respectively, 82 m.p.h. and 93 m.p.h.

**Type:** (*Tractor*) *Single-seat scout;* (*pusher*) *single-seat fighter.* **Power:** (*Tractor*) *believed to be 80-h.p. Clergetse ven-cylinder rotary engine;* (*pusher*) *80-h.p. Gnome seven-cylinder rotary or 90-h.p. Salmson M.7 seven-cylinder water-cooled radial engine.* **Armament:** *No details available.* **Performance** (*pusher scout*)*: Maximum speed (Gnome) 82 m.p.h., (Salmson) 93 m.p.h. Initial rate of climb (Gnome) 1,000 ft./min., (Salmson) 970 ft./min.* **Weights** (*pusher scout*)*: Empty (Gnome) 760 lb., (Salmson) 980 lb.; loaded (Gnome) 1,150 lb., (Salmson) 1,370 lb.* **Dimensions** (*pusher scout*)*: Span, upper 32 ft. 5 in., lower 20 ft.; length (Gnome) 23 ft. 3½ in., (Salmson) 21 ft. 11 in.; wing area (Gnome) 247.5 sq. ft., (Salmson) 253 sq. ft.*

# ROBEY-PETERS DAVIS GUN CARRIER

*The Robey-Peters Davis gun carrier photographed shortly after completion.*

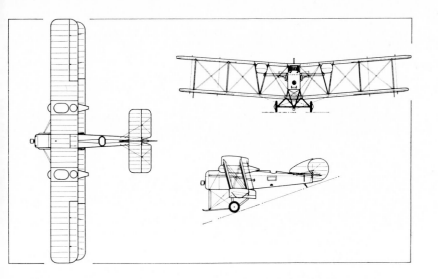

The Admiralty, doubtless mindful of the likely need to attack German airships with the most effective weapons available, evinced an early interest in the American Davis gun. This was an unwieldy weapon, its enormous length dictated by its recoilless nature, for it fired a compensating charge along an aft-facing barrel simultaneously with the forward discharge of its explosive shell from the forward barrel. The fact that it could fire explosive shells and, being free from recoil, could apparently be used with safety from the frail aircraft of the time, naturally commended it to the Admiralty.

Various experimental installations of the Davis gun were made in standard Service aircraft, and the Admiralty issued requirements for aircraft to be designed specifically to carry this gun. All the known installations of the Davis gun were single guns: it is uncertain how many were to be carried by the two different designs, one of them a triplane, prepared by the Kingsbury Aviation Co., but they may have been to the same specification that produced the remarkable three-seat biplane built by the Robey company to J. A. Peters' design. Serial numbers were allotted for two

*In this view of the aircraft the elevated gunners' positions and the impossible position of the pilot's cockpit can be seen.*

prototypes, 9498–9499, but apparently only one was built.

This cumbersome, ill-proportioned aircraft appeared in the spring of 1917. It was powered by a Rolls-Royce Eagle engine and had three-bay wings of equal span. The pilot's cockpit was impossibly far aft, as the illustrations show, and he could have had no view for landing. There was a transparent panel in each side of the cockpit. The two gunners and their guns were to be carried in two nacelles attached to the upper mainplanes.

Flight controls were conventional, and it seems likely that the trailing portions of both centre sections were hinged to act as air brakes. The undercarriage embodied a long central skid, a necessary safeguard against overturning in view of the exposed positions of the gunners.

The first attempt to fly the Robey-Peters three-seater at Bracebridge Heath was un-

successful. During the take-off run the undercarriage skid dug in and the aircraft stood on its nose. The pilot was slightly injured; fortunately, the gunners' cockpits were unoccupied. Three days later the repaired aircraft was got off the ground but crashed on the local mental hospital after making only a half circuit of the aerodrome. It was said that the crash was caused by crossed aileron controls. The pilot escaped unhurt, but the Robey-Peters three-seater was destroyed by fire and it appears that no further development was undertaken.

**Type:** *Three-seat anti-airship fighter.* **Power:** *250-h.p. Rolls-Royce.* **Armament:** *Two Davis quick-firing recoilless guns.* **Performance:** *No details available.* **Weights:** *No details available.* **Dimensions:** *Span, 54 ft. 6 in.; length, 29 ft. 9 in.; height, 12 ft. 6 in.*

## A.E.3, the R.A.E. RAM

The battles of 1917 had demonstrated the usefulness of ground-attack aircraft, but the successes of the low-flying D.H.5s, Camels, S.E.5a's and Armstrong Whitworth F.K.8s

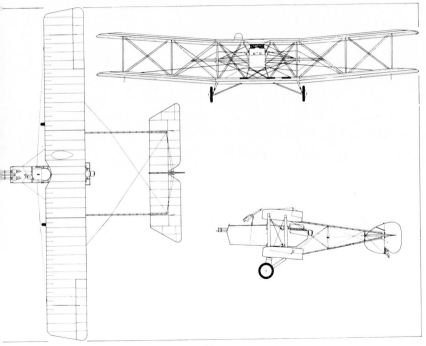

were bought at great cost in the lives of their gallant crews. The armoured B.E.2c's of No. 15 Squadron had earlier proved their ability to come through heavy ground fire but other attempts to provide some form of armour protection for the aircrews of the time had been virtually abandoned, doubtless because the weight penalty reduced performance too much.

By early 1918, however, a decision to build special-purpose ground-attack aircraft had been reached. It may have been inspired by the appearance of the German Junkers J.I armoured biplane. The Sopwith company produced their T.F.1, an armoured version of the F.1 Camel with downward-firing guns; and quickly followed this up with their T.F.2 Salamander, a thoroughly practical aircraft of good performance. For the same purpose Vickers produced the Vampire II.

Two-seaters were also wanted for ground-attack duties. Late in 1917 the Royal Aircraft Factory designed an armoured two-seater that embodied a number of N.E.1 components. The new aircraft was designated A.E.3 (presumably Armoured Experimental), its predecessors in the A.E. series having been the F.E.3, which had had the alternative designation A.E.1 but was not armoured, and the projected A.E.2 of 1917.

The original design for the A.E.3 envisaged the use of the 200-h.p. Hispano-Suiza engine. The outer wing panels, undercarriage, tail-booms, tailplane and elevators were identical with those of the N.E.1, but the nacelle, centre sections, fin and rudder were of new design. The nacelle was constructed entirely of armour plate, the rigidity of which obviated the need for any structure of longerons and spacers. Its floor and front were of double thickness, the outer armour being of 10-gauge plate, the inner of 5-gauge plate. A pair of Lewis guns were mounted on the front of the nacelle; their movement, both in azimuth and

depression, was limited. A third Lewis on a pillar mounting was provided to defend the A.E.3 against enemy fighters. There was to be provision for no fewer than thirty-two 97-round drums of ammunition.

Three prototypes, B8781–B8783, were ordered. The design was revised to have either the 200-h.p. Sunbeam Arab or the 230-h.p. Bentley B.R.2 rotary. The shape of the nacelle was slightly altered, and the mounting for the twin Lewis guns was modified to enable them to be fired almost vertically downwards. Control runs to the tail surfaces were re-arranged, and the profile of the fin and rudder was revised.

By 28th March 1918 the first A.E.3, B8781, had been completed and was sent for final inspection. It had a Sunbeam Arab engine (No. 16251), the radiator being installed between the rear centre-section struts. This position proved unsatisfactory, and by 11th April the radiator was re-sited above the centre section.

The second A.E.3 to be completed was B8783, which had the B.R.2 engine. This version had a modified stern to its nacelle and a cutaway in the trailing portion of the upper centre section; an enlarged oil tank was fitted and the main fuel tank was installed differently. By this time the Royal Aircraft Factory had been renamed the Royal Aircraft Establishment and the A.E.3 had been officially named the R.A.E. Ram; the Arab-powered aircraft was the Ram I, that with the B.R.2 the Ram II.

The last of the three Rams was B8782, which was sent for final inspection on 10th June 1918. It was a Ram I.

A series of test flights of the Ram II that began on 4th June 1918 revealed some shortcomings in control response, consequently an enlarged rudder and balanced ailerons were fitted. On 30th June B8783 went to France for Service trials. It went first to No. 201

Squadron at Noeux, where it made five flights. On 13th July it was sent to No. 209 Squadron at Bertangles, and was flown by several pilots including Captain S. M. Kinkead. Both units were ex-R.N.A.S. Camel squadrons, and their pilots are unlikely to have been enthusiastic about the ponderous A.E.3.

The Ram II returned to Farnborough on 20th July. The first Ram I had gone to Orfordness late in June 1918, doubtless for armament trials.

No development was undertaken, and the projected Ram III, a much modified derivative, was not pursued. This may have been because the Sopwith Salamander was expected to be adequate in the ground-attack rôle.

**Type:** *Two-seat ground-attack fighter.* **Power:** *(Mk I) 200-h.p. Sunbeam Arab eight-cylinder water-cooled engine; (Mk II) 230-h.p. Bentley B.R.2 nine-cylinder rotary engine.* **Armament:** *Three 0.303-inch Lewis guns.* **Performance:** *The speed of the original design with 200-h.p. Hispano-Suiza engine was estimated to be 95 m.p.h. at ground level. No further details available.* **Weights:** *No details available.* **Dimensions:** *Span, 47 ft. 10½ in.; length, 27 ft. 8½ in. (over guns); height, 10 ft.; wing area (Mk I), 560 sq. ft.*

# B.E.2c and 2e

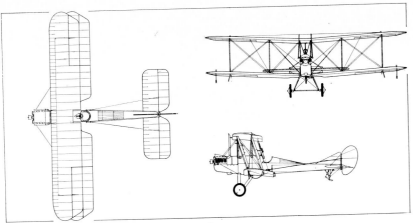

The B.E.2c was the product of Edward Busk's extensive experiments in automatic stability. At a time when this quality was thought to be highly desirable in military aircraft, which were expected to be no more than reconnaissance vehicles in the war whose imminence had to be recognised, the B.E.2c was naturally put into production. Its developmental history will be related in the appropriate companion volume.

It is curious that the B.E.2c, which proved so inadequate in aerial combat, should yet find employment in fighter rôles. It was surprisingly successful as a Home Defence fighter, was one of the earliest armoured aircraft of the war, and was used to test unusual weapons. Some of its "fighter" applications were homemade, evolved in enthusiasm, desperation, or defiance.

One of the earliest attempts to cast the B.E.2c in the fighter rôle began in the summer of 1915. Commander N. F. Usborne and Lieutenant-Commander de Courcy W.P. Ireland designed a means of attaching a B.E.2c to an S.S.-type airship envelope. The object was to remain aloft until a Zeppelin was sighted; casting off the envelope by means of quick-release devices, the B.E.2c would start its engine and attack. After preliminary trials at Kingsnorth in August 1915, flown by Flt.-

Cdr. W. C. Hicks, had revealed control weaknesses modifications were made. The next launching trial, with Usborne and Ireland aboard, was made on 21st February 1916. The airship-plane, as the combination was called, exceeded its equilibrium height; this caused a loss of gas pressure, which in turn brought about the premature release of the forward suspension of the B.E.2c. The B.E.'s nose dropped sharply and the remaining suspension wires sheared; probably the aeroplane's flying controls were damaged at the same time. Ireland was thrown out and the B.E. crashed, killing Usborne.

It was as a ground-based anti-Zeppelin aircraft that the B.E.2c, with all its limitations, scored its successes as a fighter aircraft: the type accounted for five enemy airships. The Admiralty sent a handful of B.E.2c's to R.N.A.S. aerodromes for Home Defence purposes in July 1915, and in October 1915 the sketchy aerial defences of London were reinforced by six B.E.2c's: two at Northolt, two at Hainault, and two at Sutton's farm. At the end of December it was laid down that seven more aerodromes round London were to have two B.E.2c's manned by pilots trained in night flying.

There was something to be said for this employment of the B.E.2c. Home Defence at that time meant night flying, then an extremely hazardous activity; the B.E.'s great stability reduced some of the risk and provided a steady gun platform if the target could be approached.

*The B.E.2c flown by 2nd-Lt. F. Sowrey of No. 39 Squadron when he shot down the Zeppelin L.32 on 24th September 1916. The officer on the extreme left of the group is unknown; the other four are (l. to r.) Lt. W. J. Tempest (who shot down the L.31 on 1st October 1916), Capt. Bowers, Lt. F. Sowrey and Lt. Dunston. On the B.E.2c the single Lewis gun can be seen immediately above the windscreen, and the attachment points for Le Prieur rocket tubes are discernible on the outer interplane struts.*

15

The Home Defence B.E.2c's were flown as single-seaters and had the front cockpit faired over. The British & Colonial Aeroplane Co. built ten single-seat B.E.2c's numbered 4700–4709, but when completed they were held at the Bristol works until R.F.C. operational requirements were determined. These B.E.2c's were converted into two-seaters at a cost of £50 each and some of them were used by training units. Paradoxically, all the known Home Defence single-seaters were modifications of aircraft originally built as two-seaters. These included a few B.E.2e's, such as No. 5844.

The first attack made by a B.E.2c on a German airship occurred on 31st March 1916, when 2nd-Lieutenant A. de B. Brandon overtook the crippled Zeppelin L.15 near Brentwood. After dropping Ranken darts and an incendiary bomb on his target Brandon lost sight of it. About an hour later L.15 broke her back and came down on the sea near Knock Deep.

From the spring of 1916 the B.E.2c was used increasingly on Home Defence duties from R.F.C. and R.N.A.S. stations and made several inconclusive attacks on enemy airships that summer. The first positive success was a spectacular one. Shortly after 2 a.m. on 3rd September 1916 Lieutenant W. Leefe Robinson of No. 39 Squadron, flying B.E.2c No. 2092, shot down the Schütte-Lanz S.L.11, inevitably in flames, over Cuffley. It was the first enemy airship to fall on British soil; Leefe Robinson was awarded the V.C. for his exploit.

Three weeks later the Zeppelins L.32 and L.33 met the same fate. The L.32 was shot down by 2nd-Lieutenant F. Sowrey, also of No. 39 Squadron, flying B.E.2c No. 4112; her sister ship was brought down by anti-aircraft gunfire, her fall being hastened by the repeated attacks of a B.E.2c flown by 2nd-Lieutenant A. de B. Brandon, who had earlier seen Sowrey's victim fall in flames. The Home Defence B.E.s were by this time armed with a Lewis gun firing upwards behind the trailing edge of the centre section. The drums were filled with a mixture of Brock and Pomeroy incendiary ammunition interspersed with tracer.

Three more Zeppelins were shot down by B.E.2c's: L.31 on 31st October 1916, by 2nd-Lieutenant W. J. Tempest, No. 39 Squadron, R.F.C.; L.34 shortly after 11.30 p.m. on 27th November by 2nd-Lieutenant I. V. Pyott, No.

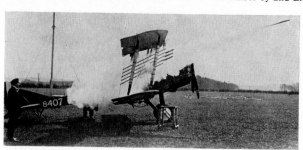

*A ground firing of Le Prieur rockets from B.E.2c No. 8407.*

*(Left) A Home Defence B.E.2e fitted with launching tubes for four rockets, flare brackets and navigation lights.*

*(Below) Armoured B.E.2c No. 2028 at Farnborough, 20th April 1916.*

(*Left*) B.E.2c (*possibly No. 1688*) *carrying two Fiery Grapnel weapons, Farnborough, 19th April 1916.*

(*Below*) *Lt. C. J. Chabot's battery of Lewis guns on a B.E.2c of No. 30 Squadron, R.F.C. Four of the five guns are seen here.*

36 Squadron, R.F.C.; and L.21 on 28th November, by Flt. Lt. E. Cadbury, Flt. Sub-Lt. G. W. R. Fane, and Flt. Sub-Lt. E. L. Pulling of R.N.A.S. Great Yarmouth. Cadbury was flying B.E.2c No. 8625, Pulling No. 8626. The victory was credited primarily to Pulling.

Several B.E.2c's and B.E.2e's of R.F.C. Home Defence units were fitted with Le Prieur rocket mountings, and the R.N.A.S. experimented with Le Prieur rockets on B.E.2c No. 8407, but there is no record of these weapons being used in combat by a B.E.

The Royal Aircraft Factory was not slow to act on requests from France for armour to protect aircrew from small-arms fire from the ground. Several schemes for fitting armour plate to the B.E.2a, 2b, and 2c were designed

and it is recorded that, as early as April 1915, the B.E.2c's Nos. 1671, 1672 and 1687 had been fitted with an armoured seat, presumably for the pilot. The first of these went to No. 6 Squadron in France and was wrecked on or about 18th April 1915, after a very brief career. No. 1687 served with Nos. 2 and 12 Squadrons for five months, but no record of any opinion on its armoured seat seems to have survived. Probably the pilots and observers preferred to do without the extra weight, for the B.E.2c's performance was poor enough at any time.

As the war intensified, contact patrol and ground-attack duties became more and more hazardous. Farnborough therefore produced a version of the B.E.2c with its engine and cock-

pits protected by armour plate. Crudely applied and weighing 445 lb., it reduced the B.E.'s performance but proved effective in service. The armoured B.E.2c's of No. 15 Squadron included trench-strafing among their activities; one of their aircraft, flown by Captain Jenkins during the battle of the Somme, was fitted with eighty new wing panels and various other components in one period of three months.

The first armoured B.E.2c was apparently No. 2028, which was at Farnborough in mid-April 1916. By the end of the first week of October 1916 a further twelve had been recorded. These were Nos. 2713–2716, 4201, 4203, 4205, 4400, 4546, 4582, 4583 and 4599. Of these, No. 2715 is known to have been in use, for training purposes, with No. 36 Reserve Squadron at Beverley in mid-1917. By then it must have lost its armour.

The Fokker menace and the lack of a British gun-synchronizing mechanism produced some extraordinary weapons. One that would have delighted Mr. Heath Robinson was the Fiery Grapnel, a fearsome anchor-like device that was to be dropped on an enemy aircraft from above, entangled firmly in its structure, and then exploded. It was tested on a B.E.2a and on the B.E.2c No. 1688 in January and April 1916.

Much more practical was the home-made installation of five Lewis guns under the fuselage of one of No. 30 Squadron's B.E.2c's. This was made by Lieutenant C. J. Chabot, using steel tubing from a crashed Farman F.27, and was intended for ground-attack work against Turkish aerodromes. When tested the gun battery worked well, but the test firing stampeded horses of the British cavalry, which were being watered near the spot chosen by Chabot for his test. On landing he was ordered by his irate C.O. to dismantle the device and return the guns to the armoury, consequently they were never fired in combat.

No. 30 Squadron had a B.E.2c, No. 4191, that was flown as a single-seater and was known in the squadron as the Scout. Its front cockpit was faired over; its speed was 88 m.p.h. at 2,000 ft. and it climbed to 10,000 ft. in 22 mins.

Also in the Middle East, possibly with No. 14 Squadron, was another single-seat B.E.2c. In this aircraft the cockpit was about midway between the positions of the two standard openings and was apparently armoured in a home-made fashion.

**Type:** *Single-seat Home Defence fighter; armoured two-seat contact-patrol and ground-attack aircraft.* **Power:** *One 90-h.p. R.A.F. 1a eight-cylinder air-cooled engine.* **Armament:** *One 0.303-in. Lewis machine-gun; some Home Defence aircraft were armed with Rankin darts, Le Prieur rockets and incendiary bombs.* **Performance:** *No figures available for Home Defence version. Armoured B.E.2c had a speed of 85.5 m.p.h. at ground level; climb to 3,500 ft., 10 min.* **Weights:** *No figures available for Home Defence version. Armoured B.E.2c weighed 2,374 lb. loaded.* **Dimensions:** *Span, 37 ft., length, 27 ft. 3 in., height, 11 ft. 1½ in., wing area, 371 sq. ft.*

# B.E.12

The original reason for building the B.E.12 is somewhat obscure. It has been long believed that the aircraft was hurriedly produced in a somewhat makeshift attempt to counter the Fokker monoplane, but history lends no support to this theory. Anthony Fokker started a tour of German operational units, demonstrating the only two Fokker E.I's then in existence, in May 1915; by mid-July only eleven Fokkers were in service on the western front; and the first combat victory scored by an E.I did not occur until 1st August 1915,

when Leutnant Max Immelmann of Fl. Abt. 62 shot down a British aircraft that was bombing Douai aerodrome.

At Farnborough, preparations to modify the Bristol-built B.E.2c No. 1697 had begun at the end of June 1915. At that date design work on the Royal Aircraft Factory's single-seat fighter, the F.E.8, was well advanced; and it can reasonably be assumed that this pusher represented the latest ideas of the Farnborough design staff on the design of single-seat fighters. By 28th July 1915, when No.

*The prototype B.E.12, No. 1697, at Farnborough, 30th September 1915. The upper longerons are straight and horizontal ahead of the cockpit, and the inverted-Y exhaust stack is a prominent feature.*

*This comparable view of a production B.E.12, No. 6478, shows the modified fuselage accommodating an enlarged petrol tank between the centre-section struts. This aircraft has the later rounded fin.*

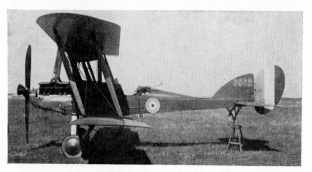

*An operational B.E.12, No. 6562, that was captured intact by the Germans. It is here seen at Aldershot, still armed with its rearward-firing Lewis gun in addition to the fixed Vickers on the port side of the fuselage.*

*The standard Vickers gun installation, showing the long connecting rod of the Vickers-Challenger interrupter gear. The pipe-like object under the cockpit is an R.L. tube (a chute for dropping anti-aircraft incendiary bombs, smoke marker bombs, signal or parachute flares), and there is an adjustable mounting for a Lewis gun ahead of the windscreen.*

1697 was sent for its pre-flight inspection, it had been converted into a single-seater and fitted with a twelve-cylinder engine that can only have been the 150-h.p. R.A.F.4, which, using R.A.F.1 engine components, had the same stroke (120 mm.) as the eight-cylinder power unit.

It therefore seems obvious that, although fighting may have been envisaged as one of the duties of the more powerful aircraft, it was not built as any kind of specific answer to the Fokker monoplane. For some weeks No. 1697 continued to be recorded as a B.E.2c; not until September 1915 does the designation B.E.12 begin to appear.

The installation of the R.A.F.4 engine in No. 1697 was made in a straightforward manner by fitting new engine bearers to the basic B.E.2c fuselage. A large pressure tank filled the fuselage space between the centre-section struts and was faired over to conform to the cross-section of the top decking. An ugly arrangement of individual exhaust pipes led to an inverted-Y stack that discharged above the centre section; there were two air-scoops above the engine, one behind the other.

No very obvious urgency appeared to attend the development of the B.E.12. By the beginning of September 1915 No. 1697 had been fitted with new exhaust pipes, and by 22nd September its original triangular fin had been replaced by a surface of greater area. Although the aircraft retained the inverted-Y form of exhaust stack it was later fitted with the single large air scoop of the production B.E.12.

During that same month the prototype had been experimentally flown on bomb-dropping and dart-dropping tests at Farnborough, exercises that seem to suggest that the B.E.12 may have been intended to be a general-purpose aeroplane, its greater power and lack of an observer enabling it to lift a greater war load

than the B.E.2c. It is also significant that all production aircraft had a camera attachment on the starboard side.

All the production B.E.12s were built in Coventry, the principal contractor for the type and its variants being the Daimler Co., Ltd., while the Standard Motor Co., Ltd., and the Coventry Ordnance Works each had a single contract. On the production aircraft the design of the forward fuselage had been revised: in front of the cockpit the upper longerons were cranked downwards to allow a larger petrol tank to be installed. An auxiliary gravity tank was fitted under the port upper wing. Power was provided by the 150-h.p. R.A.F.4a engine, the production version of the R.A.F.4 with stroke increased to 140 mm. These modifications may have first been made to the proto-

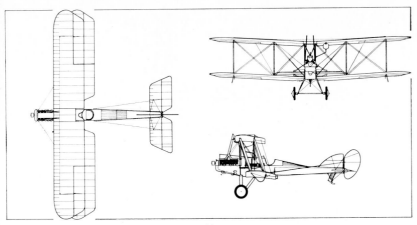

type, for it was submitted on 21st November 1915 for inspection after reconstruction.

The first R.A.F.4a engines did not come off the assembly lines until the end of 1915, and it was late in March 1916 when the first Daimler-built B.E.12 (No. 6478) arrived at Farnborough. All production aircraft had twin upright exhaust stacks. The early B.E.12s had the small triangular fin originally fitted to No. 1697, but this was soon replaced by the larger rounded fin that was standardized for all B.E. types.

It appears that the possibility of using the B.E.12 as a single-seat fighter did not begin to be explored until the spring of 1916. On 4th March, No. 1697 was inspected, having been fitted with an experimental gun mounting and an experimental airscrew. One can only guess at the nature of this experimental combination, but it may have consisted of a fixed gun and an armoured airscrew: it is certain that, fitted with a Lewis gun and deflector plates, No.

1697 was tested on 9th June 1916. Moreover, an installation of a fixed Lewis gun on the starboard side of the fuselage, firing through an armoured airscrew, was regarded as one of the standard forms of armament for the B.E.12.

Early weapon installations on the B.E.12 consisted of a single Lewis gun on a Strange oblique mounting on the fuselage side or on an overwing mounting above the centre section.

By March 1916 the Vickers mechanical interrupter gear had become available, and it was decided to fit a Vickers gun to the B.E.12 as its standard armament. It is known that the aircraft tested at the C.F.S. on 4th, 5th and 11th May 1916 had a Vickers gun with interrupter gear. The C.F.S. report boded ill for the B.E.12, however, for it stated that the aircraft manoeuvred more slowly than the B.E.2c. A combination of the Vickers interrupter gear and a Lewis gun was also devised for the B.E.12 but probably did not proceed beyond the experimental stage.

*B.E.12 with modified exhaust manifolds.*

A more ambitious scheme was tried on No. 6511 in June 1916. A Davis six-pounder recoilless gun was mounted on the starboard side of the fuselage, firing forwards and upwards at 45°. The muzzle of this cumbersome weapon was level with the leading edge of the upper wing, which had to be cut back to the front spar; and the gun had to be lowered to the horizontal for reloading. Obviously intended for anti-airship duties, the installation was clumsy and unpractical and was soon abandoned.

One B.E.12 was in France on 1st July 1916, attached to No. 10 Squadron at Chocques. The first squadron wholly equipped with the type was No. 19, which arrived at the front in France on 1st August 1916. Only one other unit, No. 21 Squadron, had B.E. 12s, completing its re-equipment by 25th August.

The B.E.12's operational career as a fighter was brief, for its lack of manoeuvrability made it useless in combat. Major-General Trenchard bluntly announced his intention of withdrawing it from fighting duties in mid-September and recommended that no more be sent to France. The B.E.12s had been used for bombing duties on several occasions, and continued to be so employed, with heavy losses, until February 1917. A few were still in service with the Special Duty Flight of the Headquarters 54th Wing in March 1918.

In the Near East and Macedonia the B.E.12 was longer-lived, and Captain G. W. Murlis-Green of No. 17 Squadron shot down several enemy aircraft while flying a B.E.12. One was still on the strength of No. 17 Squadron at the Armistice, when another was with No. 150 Squadron.

Minor modifications were made to the B.E. 12 as production progressed. The later aircraft had the smaller tail-plane with raked tips that was used on the B.E.2e, and some had deeper sump cowlings.

*A586 must, almost certainly, have been built as a B.E.12a, but is here seen with B.E.12 wings.*

Several Home Defence squadrons flew B.E.12s. On the night-flying duties that were so frequently demanded the B.E.12's stability was something of an asset, but the type still scored few successes. Its most spectacular moment came at 3.28 a.m. on 17th June 1917, when Lieutenant L. P. Watkins of No. 37 Squadron, flying No. 6610, shot down the Zeppelin L.48 at Theberton. The armament of the Home Defence B.E.12s varied a great deal, one aircraft having no fewer than four Lewis machine guns. Some had Le Prieur rockets, carried on the outer interplane struts.

Both France and Germany had experimented with aircraft covered with transparent material in the vain hope of evolving an invisible aeroplane. Similar experiments were conducted at Farnborough in January and February 1917; the subject aircraft was the B.E.12 No. 6148, its fuselage being covered with celluloid abaft the cockpit.

At least one B.E.12, C3188, was fitted with a 200-h.p. R.A.F.4d engine. This aircraft was flown at the armament experimental station at Orfordness, and in August 1918 was fitted with specially treated upper wings and ailerons in order to test pigment dope and oil varnish. **Type:** *Single-seat general-purpose aircraft.* **Power:** (*Standard*) *150-h.p. R.A.F.4a twelve-cylinder air-cooled engine; prototype had 150-h.p. R.A.F.4; at least one B.E.12 had a 200-h.p. R.A.F.4d.* **Armament:** *One fixed, synchronized 0.303-in. Vickers machine-gun, often supplemented by one 0.303-in. Lewis machine-gun behind cockpit on port side.* **Performance:** *Maximum speed 102 m.p.h. at ground level, 97 m.p.h. at 6,500 ft., 91 m.p.h. at 10,000 ft.; climb to 5,000 ft., 11 min. 5 sec.; to 10,000 ft., 33 min.; service ceiling 12,500 ft.; endurance 3 hours.* **Weights:** *Empty 1,635 lb., loaded 2,352 lb.* **Dimensions:** *Span, 37 ft.; length, 27 ft. 3 in.; height, 11 ft. 1½ in.; wing area, 371 sq. ft.*

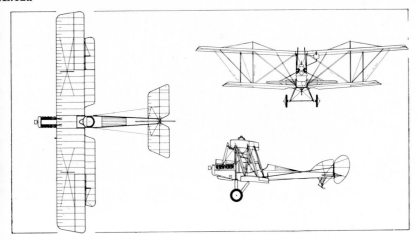

The prototype B.E.2e flew for the first time in February 1916. As this variant of the B.E.2c was ultimately built in greater numbers than any other B.E. type it was more or less inevitable that wings of the B.E.2e configuration should be mated with the B.E.12 fuselage. The resulting combination was originally designated B.E.12Ae, but common sense prevailed and the new type was soon renamed the B.E.12a.

Fewer than 100 B.E.12a's were built. The Coventry Ordnance Works and the Daimler company each received a contract for fifty; but some at least of the C.O.W.-built aircraft were built as or modified to become B.E.12s.

All had the rounded fin and small tailplane; the angle of incidence of the mainplanes was 4° 15′ (it was 4° 09′ on the B.E.12).

Central Flying School tested a B.E.12a in mid-November 1916. The report stated that, in comparison with the B.E.12, it was much easier to land, lighter on the controls, and more easily manoeuvred. No doubt Trenchard's ban on the B.E.12 was considered to cover the B.E.12a also, for no operational unit of the R.F.C. used the type in France: the few specimens that went there were flown by the Special Duty Flight of the Ninth (Headquarters) Wing for a short period in the summer of 1917.

B.E.12a's had been available in numbers

27

*Standard B.E.12a, A591. Note the camera mounting beside the cockpit*

from the late autumn of 1916 (the Coventry Ordnance Works batch of 50 had been delivered before the end of that year), and some were allotted to Home Defence squadrons before the year was out. At least three such units had B.E.12a's at some time, but the aircraft's poor climbing performance made it an unsatisfactory Home Defence machine.

In an attempt to improve the manoeuvrability of the B.E.12a, a set of experimental wings and ailerons were tested at the Royal Aircraft Factory in November 1916. These surfaces had the same basic configuration as those of the B.E.2e/12a, but their tips were raked at a wider angle and only the upper wings were fitted with ailerons. These control surfaces had very large balance areas. The

subject aircraft was No. 6511 which, as a B.E.12, had been used to test the Davis gun installation. In its modified form it did not have the gravity tank under the port upper wing that was standard on the B.E.12 and 12a.

The first recorded flight of No. 6511 in its modified form was made on 13th November 1916, with Frank Goodden at the controls. It continued to be flown in this form for at least three weeks, but the aileron balances were too large and the aircraft's flight characteristics were unpleasant. The B.E.2e wings remained standard for the B.E.12a, but the Royal Aircraft Factory revived the balanced ailerons a few months later on the F.E.9.

It was in Palestine that the B.E.12a's most active service was performed. In June 1917,

*A597 fitted with navigation lights, flare brackets, R.L. Tube and a 112-lb. bomb under the fuselage.*

*The converted B.E.12 No. 6511 with wings of B.E.12a configuration having horn-balanced ailerons on the upper main planes only.*

No. 67 (Australian) Squadron received its first B.E.12a. This aircraft's operational career was brief: in a combat with three enemy fighters on 25th June 1917 it was shot down near Tel el Sheria. On 8th July another of No. 67's B.E.12a's was forced down and its pilot, Lieutenant C. H. Vautin, taken prisoner.

When the artillery bombardment of Gaza began on 27th October 1917, No. 67 Squadron had five B.E.12a's on its strength. They were used to escort the squadron's R.E.8s, which spotted for the guns, and soon added night bombing and photography to their activities. Indeed, the only recorded victory scored by a B.E.12a occurred on 17th January 1918 during a photographic sortie, when Lieutenant L. T. E. Taplin shot down an Albatros that had attacked him.

In February 1918 No. 67 (Australian) Squadron became No. 1 Squadron, Australian Flying Corps, and handed over its B.E.12a's to the nucleus of a new R.F.C. squadron, No. 142, at Julis. By 19th September the squadron had no B.E.12a on charge, and what may have been the last two operational aircraft of the type had been destroyed. These two had been attached to Lt.-Col. T. E. Lawrence's force at El Umtaiye; one was shot down, the other destroyed by bombs.

The Royal Air Force still had sixty-four B.E.12s and 12a's on charge at 31st October 1918. More than half of that number were in the Middle East, probably at training units; only twelve were with Home Defence squadrons.

**Type:** *Single-seat fighter.* **Power:** *One 150-h.p. R.A.F. 4a twelve-cylinder air-cooled engine.* **Armament:** *One fixed, synchronized 0.303-in. Vickers machine-gun.* **Performance:** *Maximum speed 105 m.p.h. at ground level; 95.5 m.p.h. at 5,100 ft., 78.5 m.p.h. at 11,000 ft.; climb to 3,000 ft., 5 min.; to 11,000 ft., 31 min. 45 sec.* **Weights:** *Empty 1,610 lb., loaded 2,327 lb.* **Dimensions:** *Span, upper 40 ft. 9 in., lower 30 ft. 6 in.; length, 27 ft. 3 in.; height, 12 ft.; wing area, 360 sq. ft.*

## B.E.12b

By the autumn of 1917, German air raids on Britain were giving rise to considerable concern in government circles. Although the so-called silent Zeppelin raid of 19th/20th October 1917 was, from the German point of view, a failure, the most significant fact for the British home-defence organization to ponder was that none of the seventy-four aeroplanes that had taken off to attack the enemy airships was capable of climbing to the altitudes that the Zeppelins could reach with ease.

It was at precisely this time that the supply difficulties experienced with the 200-h.p. Hispano-Suiza engines were at their worst. Overhaul of Brasier-built Hispano-Suizas had been necessitated by the severe troubles stemming from faulty hardening of their reduction gearwheels; yet by October 1917 so acute was the shortage of 200-h.p. Hispano-Suizas that the engines had to be passed for service without overhaul, entries being made in their log-books that the defective gears had been left in place for want of any others. By January 1918 some 400 S.E.5a airframes, sorely needed on the western front, were lying idle in store for lack of engines.

Against this background one can assess the magnitude of the decision that created the B.E.12b. Specifically intended for Home Defence duties, this aircraft consisted of a

(*Above*) *Standard B.E.12b C*3114.

(*Left*) *B.E.12b of No. 77 Squadron with over-wing Lewis gun fitted with illuminated sights, and two 112-lb. bombs.*

B.E.12 airframe fitted with a 200-h.p. Hispano-Suiza engine; deliveries began late in 1917, and by the end of that year thirteen had been delivered to R.F.C. units. The B.E.12b's were built by the Daimler Co., Ltd.; the majority of the aircraft of the batch C3081–C3280 were of this variant.

The installation of the Hispano-Suiza closely resembled that of the S.E.5a with the same engine. Long exhaust pipes, in some

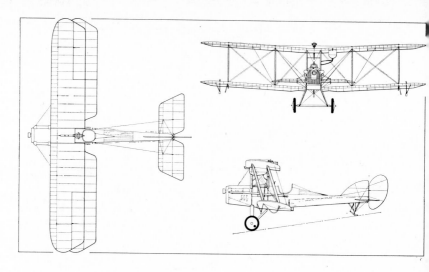

cases fitted with flame dampers, ran along the fuselage sides as far as the cockpit. The main fuel tank was a standard B.E.12/12a component but was reversed, its wedge-shaped top, which faired off the rear of the R.A.F. 4a's air scoop on the B.E.12 and 12a, facing aft.

Armament consisted of one Lewis gun fitted with Neame illuminated sights and carried on a special mounting that raised it high enough to fire over the airscrew; the gun could be swung back and down through 90° for re-loading or upward firing. At least one B.E.12b had a pair of Lewis guns on a similar mounting. Navigation lights were standard equipment and there was a Holt flare bracket under each

lower wingtip. Additional flare brackets were fitted under the tailplane or rear fuselage of some B.E.12b's: C3088 had four in this position. Several aircraft had bomb racks under the fuselage or wings to carry parachute flares and bombs.

In view of the great sacrifice that the allo-cation of the precious Hispano-Suiza engines to the B.E.12b's unquestionably was, it seems extraordinary that only thirty-six aircraft were allocated to Home Defence squadrons, twelve in 1917, twenty-four in 1918. At least four squadrons had some B.E.12b's at various times, but by 31st October 1918 only seventeen were with squadrons of the VI Brigade. A

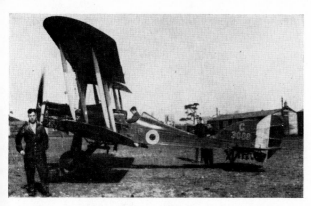

further sixty-seven were in store and thirty-one at Aeroplane Repair Depots at that date.

An official performance test report on the B.E.12b has yet to be found, but a pilot who flew the type has stated that the Hispano-Suiza engine gave it a quite spectacular performance. By the time it entered service, however, Zeppelin raids had virtually ceased and most of the squadrons using it were not near enough London to have the opportunity of intercepting the Gothas and Giants that attacked the capital and south-east England during the winter of 1917–18. This may provide part of the reason why the B.E.12b was not more widely used: it is also possible that some had to be deprived of their engines to meet the more clamant need of the S.E.5a squadrons in France.

**Type:** *Single-seat night fighter.* **Power:** *200-h.p. Hispano-Suiza eight-cylinder water-cooled engine.* **Armament:** *One 0.303-in. Lewis machine-gun; in some cases a pair of Lewis guns were fitted, and some B.E.12b's carried bombs.* **Performance:** *No figures available.* **Weights:** *No figures available.* **Dimensions:** *Span, 37 ft.; wing area, 371 sq. ft.*

## F.E.2a.

Although it has been said that the design of the F.E.2a was prepared in 1913, it seems unlikely that this was so; a confusion with the reconstructed F.E.2 seems probable. The big two-seater of January 1915 that was designated F.E.2a was, like the F.E.2, a nacelle-and-tailbooms pusher; but there was no developmental or other connexion between the two aircraft.

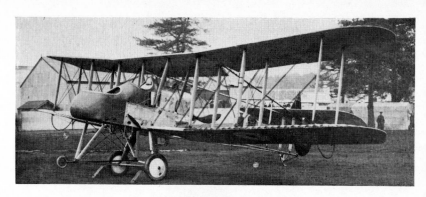

(*Above*) *The first F.E.2a with 100-h.p. Green engine*

(*Left*) *The third F.E.2a, first aircraft of the type to have the 120-h.p. Beardmore-built Austro-Daimler engine.*

The F.E.2a was probably designed in the late summer of 1914. Following the pattern that had been set by the original F.E.2 of 1912, the F.E.2a was a two-seat pusher biplane with a machine gun on a movable mounting in the front of the nacelle. The gun was a Lewis, and a simple mounting was designed for it, consisting of an angled arm pivoted centrally on the floor of the front cockpit. The underside of the nacelle was armoured.

In construction the F.E.2a was a typical Royal Aircraft Factory aeroplane, and was

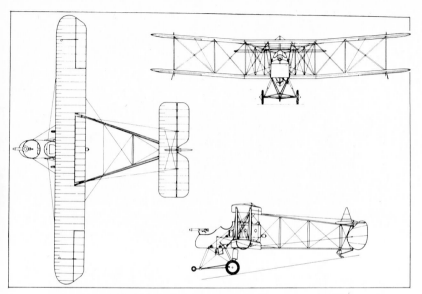

built of the conventional materials of the period. A substantial oleo undercarriage of the kind developed at the R.A.F. was fitted; it incorporated a small nosewheel to reduce the risk of overturning on landing. The mainplanes and ailerons, identical with those of the early B.E.2c, were of R.A.F.6 section; with its wide-span centre sections the F.E.2a was braced as a three-bay biplane.

The large tailplane was surmounted by the small triangular fin that characterized the F.E.2a and all its descendants. The rudder was also of characteristic profile; it was made of steel tubing.

An unusual feature of the F.E.2a was the provision of a flap-type air brake. The entire trailing portion of the upper centre section was hinged to the rear spar and could be wound down by a handwheel in the pilot's cockpit. The object of this device was to enable the aircraft to operate from the small airfields that were likely to be used in active service conditions. Even further ahead of its time was the parachute air-brake that was tested on the first F.E.2a in February 1915.

Twelve F.E.2a's were ordered off the drawing board; with the exception of the eleventh aircraft, all had the air-brake flap. The first machine was sent for its pre-flight inspection on 22nd January 1915, and made its first flight four days later, piloted by Frank Goodden. It was the only F.E.2a to have the 100-h.p. Green engine for which the type was designed. The power unit was cowled over, air intakes for the radiator being situated on each side of the pilot's cockpit. All the fuel was carried within the nacelle.

For the Beardmore engine a revised fuel system was fitted; this incorporated a gravity tank of streamline form mounted on short struts under the upper wing. A starting magneto was also provided, and the radiator air intakes were considerably enlarged.

Despite the need for military aircraft in France, production of the F.E.2a was not pressed with any real urgency. The fourth aircraft had been completed by 13th May, and the others followed on 10th June, 13th, 19th and 28th August, 7th, 13th and 23rd September and 5th October. The F.E.2a completed

*A later F.E.2a with final form of nacelle nose but retaining the streamlined gravity tank that distinguished the F.E.2a from the later F.E.2b.*

With the Green engine, which had a rather poor power/weight ratio, the F.E.2a was underpowered, and it was decided to substitute the 120-h.p. Beardmore-built Austro-Daimler, subsequently known as the 120-h.p. Beardmore. The first of the F.E.2a's to be assembled with this engine was the third aircraft, which went for inspection on 15th March 1915 and was flown by Goodden next day. Apparently the second F.E.2a had been built for the Green and had to be more extensively modified to take the Beardmore, for it was not completed until 3rd May. By that date the first aircraft had been re-engined with the Beardmore, the installation having passed inspection on 22nd April.

by 7th September was No. 12 of the series; it was fitted with B.E.2c controls.

The covering of the nacelle was progressively modified, the area of plywood being twice reduced; this probably indicated a change in the basic structure to the simpler type of nose that was standardized on the F.E.2b.

Last of the batch was No. 11, which differed from its predecessors in several respects. This F.E.2a had wings of modified section, possibly R.A.F.14, and had no air-brake flap; it was built with a plain V-type undercarriage. It flew for the first time on 7th October 1915.

At least four of the five F.E.2a's that had been completed by the end of June 1915 were in

*F.E. 2a No. 11 with V-strut undercarriage; this aircraft had no flap-type airbrake on the centre section.*

France by that date. On 30th June, Nos. 2864, 4227 and 4253 were with No. 6 Squadron, and 4293 was under repair at No. 1 Aircraft Park. Louis Strange has recorded that he flew the squadron's first F.E.2a to its aerodrome at Abeele on 20th May 1915.

It seems that No.6 Squadron was the only unit to use the F.E.2a. Louis Strange quotes a diary note of his that recorded a good opinion of the aircraft but wished for more speed, for it was not fast enough to pursue and over-take enemy aircraft that had seen it in time. Strange did a little night flying on No. 6 Squadron's F.E.2a's and found them very easy to fly at night. It may have been Strange's successful night flights that led to the fitting of dashboard lighting sets to the last few F.E.2a's.

Four F.E.2a's were still on the strength of No. 6 Squadron on 25th September 1915. During that month No. 4227 was shot down by anti-aircraft fire. Shortly after this date the first F.E.2b's began to appear and were sent to France as they became available. It is possible that No. 6 Squadron may have received a few of the first F.E.2b's in the autumn of 1915, but by mid-1916 the unit was equipped with B.E.2c's and B.E.2d's and had no F.E.s of any kind on its strength.

**Type:** *Two-seat fighter reconnaissance.* **Power:** *One 100-h.p. Green or one 120-h.p. Beardmore, both six-cylinder water-cooled engines.* **Armament:** *One 0.303-in. Lewis machine gun.* **Performance:** *(Green): Maximum speed 80.3 m.p.h. at ground level. Climb to 1,000 ft., 2 min. 45 sec.; to 3,500 ft., 9 min. 40 sec.* **Weights:** *Loaded 2,680 lb.* **Dimensions:** *Span 47 ft. 10 in., length 32 ft. 3½ in., height 12 ft. 7½ in.; wing area 494 sq. ft.*

## F.E.2b.

The F.E.2b was a slightly simplified version of the F.E.2a that was produced in quantity by firms embarking on aircraft production for the first time. The principal contractors were Boulton and Paul, Ltd. and G. & J. Weir, Ltd. The F.E.2b had no airbrake, its wing structure being identical with that of the eleventh F.E.2a; the trailing edge of the centre section therefore extended over its complete span but the chord was a little less than that of the wing panels. The absence of the air-brake flap led to a revised disposition of the elevator control cables, and a straight-sided gravity tank was attached directly to the underside of the port upper wing. As on the F.E.2a, armour plate was fitted to the nacelle.

That the design was known as early as August 1915 is suggested by a note in the Royal Aircraft Factory flight book. The first production F.E.2b, No. 5201, was at Farnborough in mid-October 1915; it was of the batch 5201-5250 ordered from Boulton & Paul. First of the F.E.2b's built at the Royal Aircraft Factory itself, No. 6328, was recorded on 3rd December 1915; but the aircraft of the first Weir-built batch 4256-4291 did not begin to appear until February 1916.

The early F.E.2b's were powered by the 120-h.p. Beardmore engine and had wings of R.A.F. 6 section.

It is probable that a few of the first F.E.2b's went to No. 6 Squadron, and it is known that at least four (Nos. 5201, 6330, 6340 and 6356) were sent to No. 12 Squadron R.F.C. in

*Built at the Royal Aircraft Factory, this early F.E.2b, No. 6341, was completed by 6th January 1916. While with No. 25 Squadron it was brought down intact by Bayerische Flieger-Abteilung 292 and is here seen in German hands.*

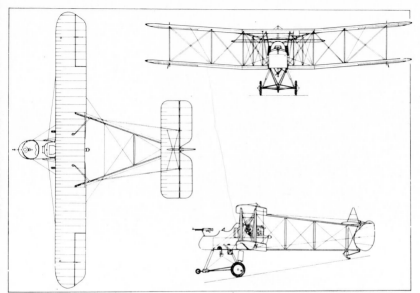

February 1916. This may have been done because of the threat to reconnaissance aircraft presented by the Fokker monoplane at that time; otherwise it was something of an anachronism, because reconnaissance squadrons had in general ceased to have a few fighting scouts on their strength and homogeneous fighting squadrons had been in existence for some time.

One of these was No. 20 Squadron, R.F.C., the first unit to be equipped throughout with F.E.2b's, which had arrived in France on 23rd January 1916. Enough F.E.s became available to equip No. 25 Squadron, which arrived in France on 20th February 1916, and Squadrons Nos. 23 and 22, which followed on 16th March and 1st April respectively.

By this time the F.E.2b design had undergone modification. Wings of R.A.F. 14 section had been standardized for the B.E.2c in place of the original R.A.F.6 surfaces; inevitably the F.E.2b was given wings of the new type also. One of the first aircraft to have the R.A.F.14 wings was No. 6354, which had been completed

*F.E.2b with nosewhee removed. This aircraft has the more-or-less standard armament of two Lewis guns, the rear one of which was on a telescopic mounting and could be fired rearwards over the upper wing.*

by 25th January 1916; Nos. 6355–6358 are known to have been similar, but the contemporary Nos. 6361–6363, 6366 and 6367 had R.A.F. 6 wings.

In an attempt to improve performance the 120-h.p. Beardmore was replaced by the 160-h.p. engine of the same make. The earliest recorded installation was made in No. 6357 which, on 21st February 1916, had 160-h.p. Beardmore No. 600. Earlier that month No. 6360 was completed with a 150-h.p. R.A.F.5 engine, and in April 1916 No. 4256 was also fitted with a R.A.F.5. This engine was a pusher version of the R.A.F.4a; a small number were built by the Siddeley-Deasy Motor Co., but

it was never developed. The two F.E.2b's Nos. 4256 and 6360 remained at Farnborough as test-bed aircraft; both were used in the series of tests of gyroscope bomb sights that started at the Royal Aircraft Factory in the summer of 1916. No. 4256 was still flying in March 1918, when it was fitted with a twin Lewis gun mounting.

References also exist to experimental installations of the 200-h.p. R.A.F.3a and 170-h.p. R.A.F.5b engines in F.E.2b's, but it is uncertain whether these were taken beyond the project stage. The R.A.F.5b was a development of the R.A.F.5 with enlarged cylinders of 105 mm. bore; one source states that this

*F.E.2b with experimental installation of RAF 5 engine.*

The F.E.2b figured in many gallant combats before and during the Battles of the Somme, possibly the best-known being the fight over Annay on 18th June 1916, when 2nd-Lieutenant G. R. Mc-Cubbin of No. 25 Squadron, with Corporal J. H. Waller as his gunner, attacked three Fokkers. One fell to Waller's fire; its pilot was Max Immelmann, one of the earliest German fighting pilots to achieve fame by his combat victories.

Various experimental installations were made in F.E.2b's. The test of gyroscope bomb sights in 4256 and 6360 have been mentioned. In May 1916, No. 6377 was fitted with a special mounting for a Vickers one-pounder quick-firing gun. The subsequent history of this aircraft is not known, but the experience gained with it probably contributed to later operational work with heavy guns. On 17th April 1917 No. 100 Squadron received two F.E.s with Vickers one-pounder guns that it used with varying success for ground-attack

engine itself was never completed.

Slow and cumbersome though it was, the F.E.2b gave a warlike account of itself; in particular it proved to be a match for the Fokker monoplane. The F.E.'s observer had an excellent field of fire in all forward directions, and the addition of one or more pillar-type gun mountings between the cockpits enabled him to fire above and behind the aircraft.

*The installation of a Harle searchlight coupled with two Lewis guns in F.E.2b A781 at Farnborough, 25th March 1917. The large wind-driven generator is conspicuous in this photograph, and there were four small landing lamps under each lower wing. The officer is Lt. W. S. Farren, later Sir William Farren, C.B., F.R.S., Hon. F.R.Ae.S.*

duties by night. An F.E.2b with a Vickers quick-firing gun was tested at Orfordness, and some others armed with this weapon were used by Home Defence squadrons.

Another attempt to fit heavier armament was made in No. 7001 in August 1916. This F.E.2b was tested at Farnborough with a 0.45-inch Maxim gun. At least two F.E.2b's used on Home Defence duties had this large-calibre Maxim gun.

An experimental installation of a R.A.F. wireless set was made in No. 4914 in June 1916; and in October No. 4928 was the test-vehicle for a searchlight designed by S. R. Whiddington of the Royal Aircraft Factory's Instruments and Wireless department. A later experiment was made in May 1917 with a Harle searchlight, which was of French manufacture. This light was mounted between two Lewis guns, the whole assembly being movable. The test aircraft was the Weir-built F.E.2b A781.

Few modifications were made to the air-frame proper, and it differed scarcely at all from that of the F.E.2a. One F.E.2b flown with inversely tapered horn-balanced ailerons that increased the overall span to 50 ft. 1 in., and in January 1917 an adjustable tailplane was fitted to No. 4846. Neither modification was developed. In squadron service the undercarriage was frequently simplified by the removal of the nosewheel and its forward V-strut; long radius rods were fitted between the axle ends and the attachment points for the deleted V-strut. This modification added one or two m.p.h. to the F.E.'s speed.

Some F.E.2b's were allotted to Home Defence squadrons from the end of 1916; these units included squadrons Nos. 33, 36, 38, 51 and 58. The F.E.'s poor rate of climb and low ceiling made it an unsatisfactory aircraft for Home Defence duties. In an attempt to improve its performance, some squadrons converted F.E.2b's into single-seaters by fairing over the front cockpit; these aircraft had one Lewis gun or, occasionally, two, fired by the pilot. A few more ambitious modifications of the type had the single pilot's cockpit midway between the two normal seats.

On these aircraft a new top decking was fitted
and the two fixed Lewis guns were carried
internally.

The arrival of the new, fast and well-armed
Albatros and Halberstadt fighters in the
autumn of 1916 was the beginning of the end
for the gallant old F.E. as a fighting aircraft.
The F.E.2b's fought on doggedly until the
spring of 1917; finally on 3rd April IV Brigade
orders said that F.E.2b aeroplanes were no
longer to be used by themselves on offensive
patrols. Thereafter the daylight use of the type
consisted mainly of photography, bombing
and line patrol work, usually under the
escort of single-seat fighters; but as late as
August 1917 the F.E.s of No. 18 Squadron
performed a good deal of ground-attack
work.

By that time the F.E.2d had long superseded
the F.E.2b in Nos. 20 and 25 Squadrons, and

No. 23 had become a single-seat squadron
equipped with Spads. The last aircraft were
superseded in August 1917, after which date
the F.E.2b's operational career continued with
night-bombing, anti-submarine and Home
Defence units; its history in the first two of
these capacities will be told in another volume
in this series. As noted above, the F.E. was
not a success as a Home-Defence aircraft
and was withdrawn early in 1918.

About 800 F.E.2b's were built for fighter-
reconnaissance duties, but when it was found
that the F.E. was well suited to night-bombing
duties production was continued into 1917
and had to be expanded again in 1918. Maximum output had been 286 in the quarter ended
30th June 1917, whereafter it diminished until
the end of the year; in the first three months of
1918 only fifteen were completed. Output went
up again during 1918, and no fewer than 202

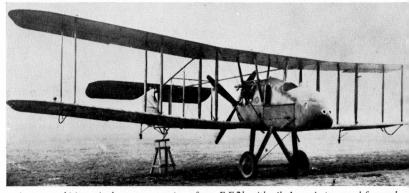

*A more ambitious single-seat conversion of an F.E.2b with pilot's cockpit moved forward and two internally mounted Lewis guns. This aircraft was used by No. 51 Squadron at Tydd St. Mary, Lincs.*

F.E.2b's were built in the last quarter of that year. It seems probable that the total output of 1,939 F.E.2b's quoted in official statistics included night bombers made by converting earlier production aircraft; certainly the official figure considerably exceeds the total represented by the batches of serial numbers allotted for the type.

Outside the night-bombing squadrons the F.E.2b ended its days at training units, teaching embryo observers their trade. Some of these aircraft (e.g., A800) had a Scarff ring on the gunner's cockpit and a V-type undercarriage of the kind standardized for the night-bomber version of the type.

**Type:** *Two-seat fighter-reconnaissance.* **Power:** *One* 120-h.p. *or* 160-h.p. *Beardmore six-cylinder water-cooled engine; experimental installation of one 150-h.p. R.A.F.5 twelve-cylinder air-cooled engine.* **Armament:** *One or two free-mounted 0.303-inch Lewis machine guns; a few aircraft had one Vickers one-pounder gun or one 0.45-inch Maxim gun. Bombs were carried for ground-attack duties.* **Performance** *(160-h.p.): Maximum speed 91.5 m.p.h. at ground level, 81 m.p.h. at 6,500 ft., 76 m.p.h. at 10,000 ft.; climb to 6,500 ft., 18 min. 55 sec.; to 10,000 ft., 39 min. 44 sec.; service ceiling 11,000 ft.* **Weights** *(160-h.p.): Empty 2,061 lb., loaded 3,037 lb.* **Dimensions:** *Span, 47 ft. 9 in., length 32 ft. 3 in., height, 12 ft. 7½ in., wing area 494 sq. ft.*

# F.E.2c.

The designation F.E.2c was applied to two different variants of the F.E.2b design. The first was an alternative fighter-reconnaissance version of the F.E.2b in which the pilot sat in the front cockpit, the gunner in the rear. The design drawings had been completed by the beginning of October 1915 and some components had been made by that time, for on 1st October an F.E.2c upper centre section was submitted for inspection after conversion to F.E.2a standard.

In its basic structure the F.E.2c nacelle did not differ from that of the F.E.2b, but the shapes of the nose fairing and the cockpit coamings were modified. The nose fairing incorporated a Lewis gun that had a limited degree of movement and was linked to a sighting bar or tube mounted immediately in front of the pilot's windscreen. This gun was fired by the pilot, the linkage ensuring that the gun was always aligned with the sight. Immediately behind the pilot's seat was a mounting for the observer's Lewis gun: this was an Anderson rear-arch mounting, a braced inverted-U member with a central pivot for the gun. The nacelle incorporated areas of armour plate.

The forward position of the pilot's seat

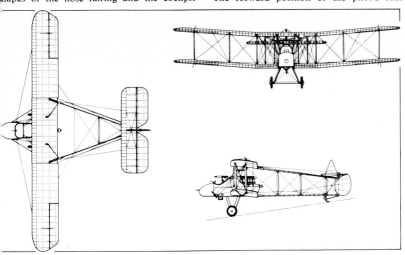

inevitably meant that the elevator and aileron cables entered the nacelle farther forward than on the F.E.2a and 2b. The F.E.2c had a plain V-type undercarriage of the type that was fitted to the eleventh F.E.2a and was to characterize the later night-bomber version of the F.E.2b. A different arrangement of access steps appeared on the F.E.2c nacelle.

Two F.E.2c's were completed in 1916. These were numbered 6370 and 6371, being the 43rd and 44th aircraft of the batch of F.E.2b's, 6328–6377, built at the Royal Aircraft Factory. No. 6371 was submitted for its final inspection on 19th March 1916, No. 6370 on the following day. Both were powered by the 120-h.p. Beardmore engine.

An early modification to No. 6370 was the substitution of the F.E.2b-type oleo undercarriage for the original V-strut assembly; this was inspected on 19th April 1916. This F.E.2c remained at Farnborough for experimental purposes. It was fitted with dual control in mid-May 1916, and in July it was used in gyroscope tests. Its career ended on 9th May 1917, when it was wrecked.

Rather less is known about No. 6371. This F.E.2c had been fitted with a new type of gun-mounting by 8th April 1916, but whether for the pilot or observer is not known. There can be little doubt that it went to France and was the F.E.2c reported to be on the strength of No. 25 Squadron, R.F.C., on 1st July 1916.

No doubt this F.E.2c's operational trials proved that the type was in no way superior to the F.E.2b, for no attempt was made to develop or produce this variant of the basic design.

In 1918 the designation F.E.2c was revived for a version of the night-bomber F.E.2b that had the pilot in the front seat and was powered by the 160-h.p. Beardmore. The necessary modifications were devised by the A.I.D., and the Royal Aircraft Factory had made a small number of the revised nacelle nose fairings by 5th May 1918, presumably for the conversion of standard F.E.2b nacelles to the new configuration. At least one F.E.2b nacelle was converted to F.E.2c standard at Farnborough later in May 1918.

One of the last production batches of bomber F.E.'s comprised the fifty aircraft H9913–H9962 ordered from Ransomes, Sims and Jeffries late in 1918. The contract required the first twelve of the batch to be F.E.2c's. The 1918 bomber F.E.2c was used by No. 100 Squadron.

**Type:** *Two-seat fighter-reconnaissance.* **Power:** *120-h.p. Beardmore six-cylinder water-cooled engine.* **Armament:** *Two 0.303-in. Lewis machine-guns.* **Performance:** *No details available.* **Weights:** *No details available.* **Dimensions:** *Span, 47 ft. 9 in., length 32 ft. 5 in. over pilot's gun; height, 12 ft. 7½ in.; wing area 494 sq. ft.*

# F.E.2d.

Although the F.E.2b proved to be surprisingly good against the Fokker monoplane fighters it lacked the performance to give chase to the speedier single-seaters. Early in 1916 an installation of the 250-h.p. Rolls-Royce engine in the F.E.2b airframe was designed; and on 4th April 1916 a proto-type, designated F.E.2d, was submitted for final inspection. This aircraft was No. 7995, and it was fitted with a 250-h.p. Rolls-Royce Mk. I (later known as Eagle I) engine, No. 1/250/31.

The first recorded flight of the prototype was made on 7th April 1916 with Frank

Goodden at the controls. On test at Central Flying School, the aircraft proved to have a top speed of 92 m.p.h. near the ground, 88 m.p.h. at 8,000 ft.; it climbed to 10,000 ft. in 32 min. 30 sec. The improvement on the F.E.2b's performance was not spectacular; nevertheless the F.E.2d was ordered in quantity. So quickly did the first of the production machines built at the Royal Aircraft Factory follow the prototype that it seems likely that production had been ordered before the prototype flew.

fitted. An early ruling that 250-h.p. Rolls-Royce Mk. I engines were to be reserved for D.H.4s, the Mk. III version for F.E.2d's, seems not to have been strictly enforced. A1 to A30 and A32 had the 250-h.p. Rolls-Royce Mk. I (225-h.p. Eagle I); A31 had the first 250-h.p. Rolls-Royce Mk. III (284 h.p. Eagle III) and this Mark was also installed in A33–A39. (A40 was used for structural testing and apparently was not fitted with an engine.) A1932 had a 250-h.p. Rolls-Royce Mk. IV (284-h.p. Eagle IV), as did twelve other F.E.

*The prototype F.E.2d, No. 7995, photographed at Farnborough on 20th April 1916.*

Three batches of F.E.2d's, totalling 85 aircraft, were built at the Royal Aircraft Factory (A1–A40, A1932–A1966 and A5143–A5152). The first, A1, was ready by 12th May 1916; A39 by 30th August 1916. Aircraft of the second batch were completed between 22nd September 1916 and 1st January 1917; A5143 was sent for its final inspection on 9th January, A5152 on 17th February 1917.

Various Marks of Rolls-Royce engines were

2d's of that batch; fifteen had the Mk. III engine, the remainder the Mk. I. In the final R.A.F.-built batch, the first seven aircraft had the 250-h.p. Rolls-Royce Mk. IV, A5150 and A5152 the Mk. I version; but A5151 was apparently the first F.E.2d to be fitted with the 275-h.p. Rolls-Royce Mk. I (322-h.p. Eagle V.)

All the other F.E.2d's were built by Boulton and Paul, Ltd., at Norwich, deliveries starting early in 1917. These aircraft were numbered within the ranges A6351–A6600 and B1851–B1900, but it is uncertain whether all were in fact F.E.2d's. It is known that A6536 was, while at the Isle of Grain, to all intents and purposes an F.E.2b; A6545 became the F.E.2h. Both may, of course, have been converted from F.E.2d's.

Engines varied, presumably in relation to availability, for Rolls-Royce engines were scarce: early in 1917 it was difficult to maintain the few F.E.2d and D.H.4 squadrons that

were in the field owing to the shortage of engines. Some F.E.2d's, like A6367, still had the 250-h.p. Rolls-Royce Mk. IV engine; later Boulton and Paul F.E.2d's, including A6371, A6372, A6373 and A6446, had the 275-h.p. Rolls-Royce Mk. II (322-h.p. Eagle VI).

The size and shape of the radiator varied considerably, and did not bear any obvious relationship to the Mark of engine fitted; A2 and A18 had a round-top radiator; A5 and A9 a square one with partial shutters; A27

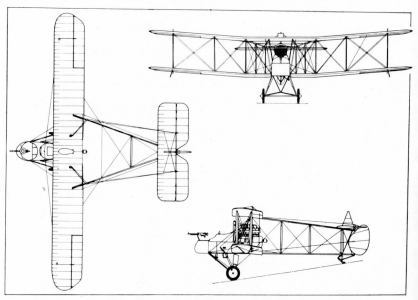

*The second production aircraft, A2, passed its final inspection at Farnborough on 17th May 1916.*

*A9 had a different form of radiator with a flat top and partial shutters.*

had a round-top radiator with quite extensive shuttering. When the round-top radiator was more or less standardized, shutters still varied in design.

On the earliest F.E.2d's the sides of the pilot's cockpit were cut right down to the upper longerons of the nacelle, but on later aircraft high coamings were fitted. Many F.E.2d's dispensed with the nosewheel of the undercarriage in an attempt to gain a few more m.p.h.

The F.E.2d was never quite the surprise to enemy fighters that it might have been. One of the first to go to France, A4, landed at Lille behind the German lines on 1st June 1916 owing to an error of navigation by its pilot, Lieutenant Organ, and the new type's secrets were in the hands of the enemy before it had fired a shot in anger.

So was an early specimen of the 250-h.p. Rolls-Royce Mk. I, for the F.E.2d was the first aircraft powered by the engine to go to France.

The hapless A4 was followed to France by other F.E.2d's, and by 1st July 1916 No. 20 Squadron had discarded its F.E.2b's and had thirteen F.E.2d's on its strength. This was the only squadron operating the F.E.2d during

*A later F.E.2d, A6355, with the high coaming round the pilot's cockpit and nose-wheel removed.*

the second half of 1916, but on 16th December No. 57 Squadron arrived from England equipped throughout with the type. By the end of the year sixty-seven F.E.2d's had gone to France; they were followed by a further 116 in 1917.

The F.E.2d gave a good account of itself (it was described by the official historian as a "more formidable type of aeroplane than the Sopwith" 1½ Strutter) until the spring of 1917. During April of that year the R.F.C. suffered severe casualties, among them the crews of several F.E.2d's, for the type was by then beginning to be outclassed. No. 25 Squadron was re-equipped with F.E.2d's in that month, but flew the type for little more than three months before changing over to D.H.4s in July. No. 57 had exchanged its F.E.2d's for D.H.4s in the preceeding month, consequently it was with No. 20 Squadron alone that the F.E.2d battled on, not unsuccessfully, until replaced by the redoubtable Bristol F.2B in the autumn of 1917.

This unit could claim several distinctions for its F.E.2d's. Sergeant Thomas Mottershead was flying A39 on 9th January 1917 when he brought it down from 9,000 ft. in flames to save the life of his observer. Mottershead was trapped in the aircraft when it crashed. His supreme act of self-sacrifice earned a posthumous V.C.

Karl Schaefer, one of Germany's leading fighter pilots, was shot down by an F.E.2d of No. 20 Squadron on 5th June 1917; and on 6th July Manfred von Richthofen was brought down wounded by another aircraft of the same squadron.

In operational service various arrangements of armament were tried, including one or sometimes two fixed Lewis guns fired by the pilot. Bomb racks were fitted, for towards the end of its career the F.E.2d did duty as a bomber on several occasions.

Twenty-three F.E.2d's were allotted to Home Defence units in 1917, two in 1918. Squadrons Nos. 33, 36 and 78 each had a few,

the aircraft being fitted with navigation lights and flare brackets. The F.E.2d's performance, although better than that of the F.E.2b, did not suffice for anti-airship duties, consequently its development as a Home Defence fighter was not pursued.

**Type:** *Two-seat fighter-reconnaissance.* **Power:** *One 250-h.p. Rolls-Royce Mk. I, Mk. III, Mk. IV; 275-h.p. Rolls-Royce Mk. I, Mk. II: all were twelve-cylinder water-cooled engines.*

**Armament:** *One or two fixed 0.303-in. Lewis machine-guns; one or two free Lewis guns; six 20-lb. or 25-lb. bombs.* **Performance:** *(250-h.p. Rolls-Royce Mk. I): Maximum speed 94 m.p.h. at 5,000 ft., 88 m.p.h. at 10,000 ft.; climb to 5,000 ft., 7 min. 10 sec.; to 10,000 ft., 18 min. 20 sec.; service ceiling 17,500 ft.* **Weights:** *(250-h.p. Mk. I.): Empty 2,509 lb., loaded 3,469 lb.* **Dimensions:** *Span, 47 ft. 9 in., length, 32 ft. 3 in., height, 12 ft. 7½ in.; wing area, 494 sq. ft.*

# F.E.6

A considerable amount of mystery surrounds the F.E.6; indeed its existence was for long regarded as doubtful. There is now no doubt that it was built and flown, but its early abandonment suggests that it was not regarded as a success. The reason for its failure is not far to seek.

In 1913 the Royal Aircraft Factory had conducted experiments with a Coventry Ordnance Works one-pounder quick-firing gun installed in the F.E.3. In these trials the F.E.3 had been slung from the roof trusses of a hangar at Farnborough; apparently no attempt

was made to fire the gun from the aircraft in flight. Within their limitations, the tests were regarded as successful.

The F.E.3 itself was a remarkable biplane powered by a 100-h.p. Chenu engine, its tail unit being carried on a single central boom the securing member of which passed through the hollow airscrew shaft. Cables braced the tail unit to the wing cellule.

In the early summer of 1914 the F.E.6 was designed. It was a two-seater specifically intended to carry a one-pounder quick-firing gun, which was to be fitted on a movable

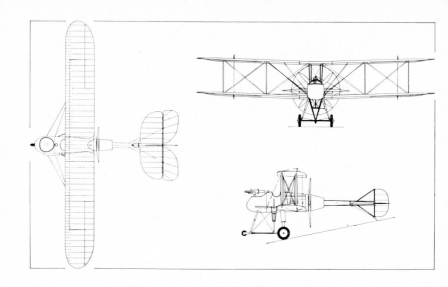

mounting in the front cockpit of the nacelle. In basic configuration it resembled the F.E.3, for it was a pusher with a single tailboom secured through the hollow airscrew shaft. On the F.E.6, however, all loads were carried by the securing member; no relief was provided by any form of bracing to any other part of the airframe. In view of the limitations imposed by the materials and techniques available at the time, it seems remarkable that the designers expected to achieve success with the F.E.6.

It was an ill-proportioned two-bay biplane with equal-span wings and ailerons at all four wing tips; the wing panels and ailerons were standard R.E.5 components. The basic structure of the nacelle was of steel tubing, the rear ends of the longerons being attached to a pair of substantial trunnions that held the forward end of the central member of the tail boom. A large fairing was attached immediately behind the airscrew; the contours of the nacelle were faired out, much as on the reconstructed F.E.2. A rather tall oleo undercarriage, incorporating a small nosewheel, was fitted.

*A static loading test on an F.E.6 tail unit. A second tail boom can be seen on the floor under the test rig. This photograph is dated 12th September 1914.*

All control cables to the rudder and elevators passed down the centre of the tail boom and emerged through the aluminium fairing of the boom some distance ahead of the leading edge of the tailplane. The tailplane was a lifting surface and had marked undercamber.

It is uncertain how many F.E.6s were originally envisaged. Some components for a second aircraft were made, but it seems that only one was built. Major components were being statically tested in mid-September 1914.

Only one entry in respect of "F.E.6 No. 1" appears in the Farnborough flight book. This is dated 24th November 1914, on which date Frank Gooden flew it for 45 minutes; it is also recorded that the undercarriage was damaged. This does not necessarily mean that the recorded flight was the first or only flight

made by the F.E.6, but it is doubtful whether it flew again, Its wings and ailerons were returned to store as standard R.E.5 spares on 27th February 1915.

The F.E.6 was over-ambitious structurally and would have been a dangerous aeroplane. Its directional control must have been unsatisfactory, for the fin and rudder looked inadequate to balance the large forward side area of the deep nacelle.

**Type:** *Two-seat heavy-gun carrier.* **Power:** *120-h.p. Austro-Daimler six-cylinder water-cooled engine.* **Armament:** *One Coventry Ordnance Works quick-firing gun.* **Performance:** *No details available.* **Weights:** *Empty (with gun) 2,000 lb.; loaded 2,650 lb.* **Dimensions:** *Span, 49 ft. 4 in.; length, 29 ft. 6 in.; height, 15 ft.; wing area 542 sq. ft.*

# F.E.8.

The F.E.8 was quite a commendable attempt by the Royal Aircraft Factory to produce a single-seat fighter, but the type seemed to be dogged by bad luck and was never able to make a name for itself. Design work was begun in the early summer of 1915 under J. Kenworthy, and the first prototype, No. 7456, was submitted for its pre-flight inspection on 14th October 1915. It flew for the first time on the following day, piloted by Frank Goodden.

For want of a gun-synchronizing gear the F.E.8 was designed as a pusher. It was quite a handsome and well-proportioned two-bay biplane with high-aspect-ratio wings; the ailerons ran the full length of the outer wing panels. One of the least satisfactory features of the aircraft was the design of the tail unit. The tail booms converged to meet on the main spar of the tailplane; the tail skid was built into the rudder, which therefore had to accept landing shocks and support the weight of the aircraft when on the ground.

built up of steel tubing, to which were attached light frames. Over these were fitted aluminium panels and the aluminium nose portion; the design included provision for the fitting of armour plate to protect the pilot. The engine was a 100-h.p. Gnome Monosoupape, driving a four-blade airscrew, which had the unusual refinement of a large conical spinner.

A peculiar position had been chosen for the Lewis gun that constituted the F.E.8's armament, the installation being very similar to that of the F.E.2c. The gun was mounted in the extreme nose of the nacelle and had a limited range of movement. It was linked to a sighting bar that was controlled by the pilot by means of a pistol grip; movement of the sighting bar to keep it on the target or aiming point produced a corresponding movement of the gun.

After preliminary trials at Farnborough the first prototype was flown to C.F.S. on 8th

*The first prototype F.E.8, No. 7456, before its Lewis gun was fitted. The nacelle was still unpainted when this photograph was taken on 14th October 1915.*

All flight surfaces were of conventional construction and were fabric covered. The nacelle, remarkably enough, was an all metal structure; it had a simple basic girder member

November 1915 by Frank Goodden for its official performance tests. Its recorded maximum speed was 94.5 m.p.h. at ground level.

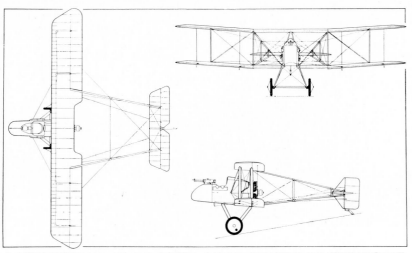

*By 11th November the Lewis gun had been installed in the nose of the nacelle and the aircraft had been doped with P.C.10 dark khaki. In the cockpit, Frank Goodden.*

The first F.E.8 was flown back to Farnborough on 15th November 1915 by B. C. Hucks. Unfortunately it was badly damaged in a landing mishap and required extensive repairs. The second prototype, No. 7457, was well advanced at this time and was mounting and was level with the pilot's eyes; external racks for spare ammunition drums were fitted. In France, No. 7457's flying time is known to have been at least 102 hrs. 46 min., for that total was recorded by No. 1 Aeroplane Depot.

*The second prototype, 7457, showing the large pointed spinner originally fitted to both prototypes.*

inspected on 3rd December 1915. Like its predecessor it was powered by the 100-h.p. Gnome Monosoupape and had a large conical spinner. The Lewis gun was again mounted in the extreme nose of the nacelle.

Goodden flew No. 7457 on speed tests on 16th and 18th December, reaching 97.4 m.p.h. on the latter date. On 19th December he flew the second F.E.8 to France for operational evaluation. For a time it was with No. 5 Squadron, and it has been recorded that this F.E.8 was favourably reported on by Service pilots, but its ultimate fate is not known; it does not reappear in the Farnborough records. It was modified at some stage in its career to the same configuration as production F.E.8s. Its gun was carried on an elevating pillar

The first prototype had been rebuilt by the beginning of April 1916 and had been passed for flight on the 6th of that month. It made its first flight after reconstruction on 9th April and thereafter was flown regularly until early 1917. The spinner had been discarded and the installation of the gun modified. The Lewis was now on a mounting immediately in front of the pilot's face, and racks outside the cockpit held spare ammunition drums.

In May 1916 No. 7456 was fitted with a 110-h.p. Clerget engine, probably because this power unit would have been a suitable alternative in the event of any failure in deliveries of Monosoupapes. Perhaps for the same reason, at least one experimental installation of a 110-h.p. Le Rhône was made in an

*No. 7457 brought up to production standard, with Lewis gun on front of cockpit and external racks for spare ammunition drums.*

F.E.8. Tests of the Le Rhône-powered aircraft were flown at C.F.S. in April 1916, and there seems no reason to doubt that No. 7456 was the subject aircraft for that installation also. Installations of the 80-h.p. Le Rhône, 80-h.p. Clerget, and 80-h.p. Gnome Monosoupape were also designed but it is unlikely that any F.E.8 was fitted with these engines.

The serial numbers 3698–3690 had been allotted for F.E.8s for the R.N.A.S. The allocation was cancelled, however, and the aircraft were not delivered.

The type was ordered in quantity from the Darracq Motor Engineering Co. Ltd., whose contracts ultimately totalled 245 aircraft, and from Vickers Ltd., who built their fifty F.E.8s at their Weybridge works. A series of setbacks retarded production seriously, and the first F.E.8s did not appear until May 1916. The first Darracq-built machine, No. 6378, was at Farnborough on 24th May; the first Vickers-built aircraft (7595) not until 1st July. The production F.E.8s were virtually identical with the rebuilt No. 7456.

Two of the first production machines went to No. 29 Squadron, R.F.C., on 15th June 1916, possibly because the F.E.8 was generally similar to the D.H.2 with which the unit was equipped. One of these aircraft was No. 6378, and it gave the F.E.8's operational career an inauspicious start, for it was shot down on 22nd June.

Production aircraft did not start coming along in appreciable quantities until July, and no other F.E.8s were sent to France until one Flight of No. 40 Squadron went there on 2nd August 1916, followed by the other two Flights on 25th August: this squadron was equipped throughout with the type.

Early experience with the F.E.8 had not been happy and several spinning accidents had occurred. Spinning was not understood at that time, and there was no recognised method of recovering from a spin. On 23rd August 1916, Frank Goodden deliberately spun an F.E.8 three times to each side and regained control by the method that has remained standard practice since that date.

With what had threatened to be a bogy convincingly laid by Goodden's courageous demonstration, the F.E.8 became quite well liked as an aircraft. The C.F.S. report on the Le Rhône-powered machine had described it as comfortable to fly and very stable. Its

57

stability did not deprive it of manoeuvrability, but its flying qualities have been described as being, in general, not quite so good as those of the D.H.2.

The F.E.8 never achieved much distinction. No. 40 Squadron brought its little pushers into the arena a full six months later than No. 24 Squadron had taken its D.H.2s to war; and six months was a long time by the standards of the 1914–18 war. The first Sopwith Pup and triplane had been in France for several weeks before the F.E.8s arrived, and indicated clearly what the immediate future held. The days of the pusher were numbered.

The F.E.8s of No. 40 Squadron fared quite well at first. Captain D. O. Mulholland shot down a Fokker monoplane and was credited with probably crashing another on 20th October 1916; next day Captain T. Mapplebeck shot down a Roland. Two days later the squadron shot down five enemy aircraft and earned the congratulations of Major-General Trenchard.

By the time the second F.E.8 squadron, No. 41, reached France on 21st October 1916,

new German fighters of high performance with heavy armament were coming into service. These outclassed the F.E.8 and D.H.2, but the pushers had to soldier on until well into 1917. On 9th March 1917 nine F.E.8s of No 40 Squadron were attacked by five Albatros scouts of *Jagdstaffel* 11 led by Manfred von Richthofen. Four of the F.E.s were shot down, four were sent down damaged, and the last caught fire while landing.

A few of No. 41 Squadron's aircraft were used on ground-attack duties in the early stages of the Battle of Messines, which began on 7th June 1917. By then No. 40 Squadron had been re-equipped with Nieuports, but with No. 41 the F.E.8 carried on until July, thereby earning the doubtful distinction of being the last pusher fighter in service in France.

Two F.E.8s were sent to Home Defence squadrons in 1917, but the type was not adopted for these duties. The F.E.8 was not apparently much used for experimental or development work. The only recorded experimental modification was tested in December

*Standard production F.E.8, No. 6390 built by Darracq.*

1916, when No. 7456 was flown at Farnborough with what were referred to as de Havilland elevators. The precise nature of this modification and the results of the tests have still to be discovered.

**Type:** *Single-seat fighter.* **Power:** *One 100-h.p. Gnome Monosoupape, 110-h.p. Le Rhône or 110-h.p. Clerget nine-cylinder rotary engine.* **Armament:** *One 0.303-inch Lewis machine gun.* **Performance:** *Maximum speed at ground level, 94 m.p.h. with Monosoupape, 93.6 m.p.h. with Le Rhône, 97 m.p.h. with Clerget; at* 10,000ft., 89 m.p.h. with Le Rhône. Climb to 5,000 ft., 7 min. 30 sec. with Monosoupape; to 6,000 ft., 8 min 20 sec. with Le Rhône; to 10,000 ft., 17 min. 30 sec. (Monosoupape); 17 min. 15 sec. (Le Rhône). Service ceiling 14,500 ft. (Monosoupape). Endurance 2½ hours (Monosoupape). **Weights:** (Monosoupape) empty 895 lb., loaded 1,346 lb.; (Le Rhône) empty 960 lb., loaded 1,470 lb.; (Clerget) loaded 1,390 lb. **Dimensions:** Span, 31 ft. 6 in.; length, 23 ft. 8 in.; height, 9 ft. 2 in.; wing area, 218 sq. ft.

# F.E.9.

*The first F.E.9, A4818, photographed on 19th May 1917.*

It appears that the design of the F.E.9 was not begun until the late summer of 1916, and it is surprising that, at such a late stage in the war, the Royal Aircraft Factory should have designed a pusher aircraft for fighter-reconnaissance duties. By that time practical British synchronizing gears for machine-guns were in use, and it was evident that tractor types generally were in performance superior to pushers.

The F.E.9 was, by 1916 standards, compact for a two-seater; and the design staff at Farn-

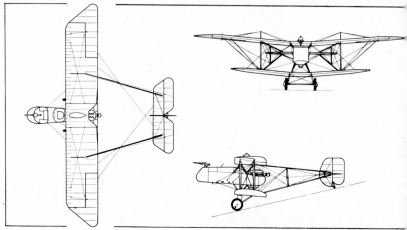

borough probably hoped that the use of the 200-h.p. Hispano-Suiza engine would ensure a performance at least comparable with contemporary types, while retaining the pusher's excellent field of fire for the observer's gun. To this end, the nacelle was carried high in the interplane gap and was connected to the upper and lower centre sections by steel-tube N-struts. This arrangement enabled the observer to fire rearwards over the upper wing.

When the first F.E.9 was completed early in April 1917 it closely resembled the preliminary layout of the design that had been drawn up in September 1916. The unequal-span wings had single-bay bracing and the enormous extensions of the upper mainplanes were cable-braced, their landing wires being attached to inverted-V kingposts directly above the interplane struts. Ailerons were fitted to the

upper wings only and had unusually large horn balances, similar to those fitted to the modified B.E.12a No. 6511.

The fin was considerably larger than the original design had envisaged. The tailskid was mounted at the lower end of the rudder post, as on the S.E.5 and R.E.8; it was in fact a modified R.E.8 component. The main undercarriage was a neat, sturdy oleo structure attached to the spars of the lower centre section.

Dual control was provided. There were two control columns side-by-side in the observer's cockpit; of these the left-hand one actuated the rudder in lieu of a rudder bar. Presumably it was feared that the observer might, in combat, stand on or obstruct the movement of a conventional rudder bar. The incidence of the tailplane could be varied in flight.

60

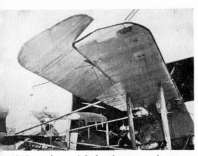

*A4818 with modified ailerons and experimental rudder, 24th October 1917.*

Two pillar-type Lewis-gun mountings were fitted, one on the front of the forward cockpit, the other behind it. The latter was provided to enable the observer to fire rearwards over the top wing.

The first F.E.9, A4818, underwent its preflight inspection on 4th and 5th April 1917. At that early stage it had been decided to build a small production batch, and work on some components was already in hand. Serial numbers were allotted for three prototypes (A4818–A4820) and twenty-four production F.E.9s (A4821–A4844). By mid-July at least twenty-four F.E.9 nacelles had been made at the Royal Aircraft Factory.

But flight trials of A4818 were not satisfactory. The climbing performance was particularly poor, and the aircraft's handling characteristics were unpleasant. This was attributable to the fact that the balance areas of the ailerons were too large, but it was thought at the time that part of the blame lay

with the rudder, which was regarded as insufficiently powerful.

Nevertheless, A4818 went to France on 6th June 1917. It was flown by a number of R.F.C. pilots at No. 1 Aircraft Depot, St. Omer, and also visited No. 56 Squadron at Liettres on 13th June. The F.E.9 was subjected to a series of tests at St. Omer, one of them with an experienced artillery observer in the front cockpit. The reports of these tests were not unfavourable, but they were so lacking in enthusiasm that Major-General H. M. Trenchard recommended that development of the type should be discontinued.

After its return to Farnborough A4818 was fitted with a new, balanced rudder and was flown extensively, with progressive modifications to the tail unit, in a series of flight tests with the object of improving its controllability. Finally, in October 1917, it had a balanced rudder of peculiar profile, and modified ailerons with smaller balance areas. This first F.E.9 continued to be flown on experimental work at least until the end of March 1918.

The ailerons that had finally been fitted to A4818 were in fact the third type to be designed for the F.E.9 and were known as Type C ailerons. They proved to be by far the best of the three designs used on the F.E.9.

The Type B ailerons were fitted to the second F.E.9, A4819, which had been completed by 16th October 1917. This aircraft had two-bay bracing for its mainplanes, which enabled it to dispense with the king-posts above the upper wing. It had a balanced rudder similar to the second surface fitted to A4819, and its tailplane appeared to be fixed. On 15th December 1917 this F.E.9 was handed over to No. 78 Squadron, a Home Defence unit at Biggin Hill, but its subsequent activities and fate are unknown.

By 1st November 1917, the third prototype,

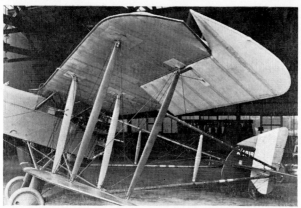

A4820, was finished. Like its immediate predecessor, it was rigged as a two-bay biplane. New ailerons and a new gravity tank had been fitted by 20th November, and the aircraft appears occasionally in Farnborough records until 23rd January 1918. It had undergone performance tests on the previous day.

No attempt to press the manufacture of the twenty-four production F.E.9s was made. No doubt Trenchard's justified condemnation of the type was sufficient to seal its fate, but the design provided the basis for the N.E.1 and A.E.3.

**Type:** *Two-seat fighter-reconnaissance.* **Power:** *One 200-h.p. Hispano-Suiza eight-cylinder water-cooled engine.* **Armament:** *Two 0.303 in. Lewis machine-guns.* **Performance:** *Maximum speed 105 m.p.h. at ground level; climb to 5,000 ft., 8 min. 25 sec.; to 10,000 ft., 19 min. 50 sec.; service ceiling 15,500 ft.* **Weights:** *Loaded; 2,480 lb.* **Dimensions:** *Span, upper 40 ft. 1 in. (Type A ailerons), 37 ft 9½ in. (Type C ailerons); lower 29 ft 5¼ in.; length 28 ft. 3 in.; height 9 ft. 9 in. Wing area 365 sq. ft.*

# N.E.1

While the first F.E.9 was undergoing its test flights the design staff of the Royal Aircraft Factory were at work on a night-fighter development with the designation F.E.12.

This design embodied several F.E.9 components, including the centre-sections, under-carriage, tailbooms, fin, rudder, and gravity tank of the earlier design; the nacelle was also

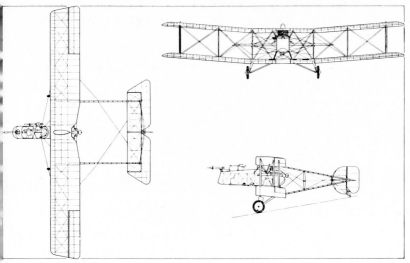

basically an F.E.9 unit, and the engine was to be a 200-h.p. Hispano-Suiza.

The F.E.12 was designed with three-bay wings of equal span, and the tailplane was correspondingly larger than that of the F.E.9. The pilot occupied the front cockpit, presumably to give him the best possible view of his target. He was to be provided with a forward-ring Lewis gun, but the main weapon was a Vickers rocket gun, fired by the observer, for which two elevated mountings were provided, one for forward firing, the other for firing to the rear.

Two searchlights are shown in the design drawings of the F.E.12: one let into the nose of the nacelle, the other on the forward mounting for the rocket gun. Power for these lights was to be provided by a wind-driven generator under the nacelle.

The design was modified and renamed N.E.1, or Night-flying Experimental. The shape of the wing-tips was altered and wide-span centre sections introduced; the tailbooms were made almost parallel in plan and were modified to bring the tailplane on to the thrust line; the searchlight on the forward gun-mounting was discarded; and the area of the fin was increased. An alternative to the F.E.9 undercarriage was designed, being a wide-track divided-axle structure.

*The first N.E.1, B3971, in its original form at Farnborough, early September 1917.*

Six prototypes, numbered B3971–B3976, were ordered. The first of these was completed by 3rd September 1917, when it underwent its final inspection. By the time B3971 emerged the design had again been modified: the fin was semi-circular, the tail booms were exactly parallel in plan, and the elevators had large horn-balance areas. The wide-track undercarriage was fitted, and the pilot occupied the front seat.

It seems that the N.E.1 first flew on 8th September 1917, that it was damaged at Brooklands on 14th September, and that it was then reconstructed. A new nacelle of constant width was fitted, the searchlight was removed, and the observer was accommodated in the front cockpit, where he could use the rocket gun more effectively. A fixed Lewis

*Side view of the same aircraft.*

64

gun, fired by the pilot, was mounted externally on the starboard side. Full dual control was fitted. The reconstruction was finished by 2nd October 1917, and the aircraft flew again two days later. After a series of test flights at Farnborough, B3971 went to Martlesham Heath on 6th November 1917.

Martlesham was not enthusiastic about the N.E.1. The official report doubted whether its performance was good enough to make it suitable for night-fighting duties, but thought it might be a slight improvement on the F.E.2b as a night-bomber. The report described the N.E.1 as "very heavy and awkward on controls, but easy to fly and land, and is very stable". The view from the cockpits and the field of fire were regarded as excellent.

Despite the N.E.1's poor reception at Martlesham all six prototypes were built. The second was inspected on 14th November 1917, the third nine days later. After brief testing at Farnborough B3972 went to Sutton's Farm, then the base of No. 78 (Home Defence) Squadron, R.F.C. What it did there and its fate were unknown.

The third N.E.1 was fitted with a modified fin that had a larger area below the tailplane than above. In February and March 1918 this aircraft was used in bomb-dropping experiments, and was also flown at Orfordness in April and May.

The fourth airframe, B3974, was subjected to structural testing and was never flown. The fifth, inspected on 21st December 1917, had no armament fitted while it was at Farnborough.

It was flown at the Isle of Grain and at the experimental armament station at Orfordness, however, and may have been used as a flying test-bed for experimental armament installations.

It is doubtful whether B3976 ever had an engine and airscrew installed. The completed airframe was inspected on 22nd January 1918, but nothing more seems to have been done with it.

The N.E.1 represented quite a commendable attempt to provide a well-equipped night fighter. Reasons for its non-adoption have never been stated, but its undistinguished climbing performance and low service ceiling handicapped it severely and it could not have reached the enemy airships that it had been primarily designed to attack. Given an engine like the Rolls-Royce Eagle VIII it might have had an acceptable performance.

**Type:** *Two-seat night fighter.* **Power:** *200-h.p. Hispano-Suiza eight-cylinder water-cooled engine.* **Armament:** *One Vickers rocket gun, one or two 0.303-in. Lewis machine-guns.* **Performance:** *Maximum speed 95 m.p.h. at 5,000 ft.; 89 m.p.h. at 10,000 ft. Climb to 5,000 ft., 9 min.; to 10,000 ft., 22 min. Service ceiling 17,500 ft.* **Weights:** *empty 2,071 lb.; loaded 2,946 lb.* **Dimensions:** *Span, 47 ft. 10½ in.; length, 28 ft. 6 in. (searchlight removed); height 10 ft. Wing area 555.1 sq. ft.*

# S.E.2

The S.E.2 was a direct derivative of the first aircraft in the world to be built to the single-seat high-speed scout formula that provided the basis for the single-seat fighters of the 1914–18 war. This progenitor was the B.S.1, a remarkably clean little biplane powered by a 100-h.p. Gnome two-row rotary. The B.S. (Bleriot Scout) category of Army Aircraft Factory designation had existed since Nov-

ember 1911, but it seems that work on the design of the B.S.1 did not start until the summer of 1912. Most of the design work was done by Geoffrey de Havilland.

The completed B.S.1 appeared early in 1913. On test it proved to have an outstanding performance: its maximum speed was 92 m.p.h., its initial rate of climb 900 ft./min. Directional control was not satisfactory, however, and a

*The S.E.2 in its original form, 11th October 1913.*

66

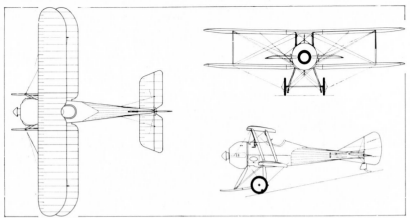

new and enlarged rudder was designed. While this new surface was being made, Geoffrey de Havilland continued to fly the B.S.1 with the original rudder. On Thursday 27th March 1913 he put the aircraft into a turn that was somewhat sharper than usual; the cantilever rudder broke over at the fuselage owing to a faulty weld; and the B.S.1 crashed. Lt. de Havilland sustained a fractured jaw.

The aircraft was rebuilt and reappeared in the autumn of 1913. By June 1913 the designation S.E.2 had come to be applied to the redesigned aircraft, the initial letters signifying Scout Experimental. (S.E.1 had been an unsuccessful canard type of 1911; in its designation S.E. had stood for Santos Experimental.) In general appearance the S.E.2 closely resembled the B.S.1, having a similar clean semi-monocoque fuselage and single-bay wings. The engine was an 80-h.p. Gnome

single-row nine-cylinder rotary, carried on a fore-and-aft mounting deep within a long-chord cowling.

The wings of the S.E.2 were virtually identical with those of the B.S.1, having the same elegant elliptical tips. Wing warping was employed for lateral control. The extremities of the lower wing had plywood covering in lieu of wing-tip skids. The tail unit was completely redesigned, having divided elevators, a small fin and a high-aspect-ratio rudder of characteristic profile. The semi-circular tailplane was a lifting surface and had distinct undercamber. An unsatisfactory feature of the design was the use of the bottom of the rudder as the tailskid: it was shod and the whole rudder had a short vertical travel against a coil spring on the rudder post. The rudder itself had an all-metal frame of steel tubing and mild-steel ribs.

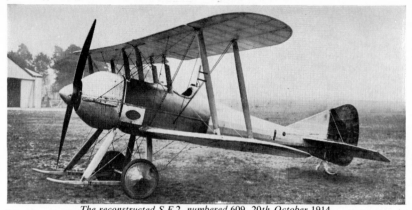
*The reconstructed S.E.2, numbered 609, 20th October 1914.*

The S.E.2 was being flown by Geoffrey de Havilland in October 1913, but its activities during the winter of 1913–14 are obscure. In the week ending 13th March 1914 it was flown to Netheravon by Major J. F. A. Higgins, but apparently it stood there unflown until Higgins flew it back to Farnborough early in April.

On its return to the Royal Aircraft Factory it was again rebuilt. The work occupied the summer of 1914, and it seems that the aircraft did not re-emerge until the beginning of October. The wings and forward portion of the fuselage of the original S.E.2 had been retained, but the rear fuselage was now a fabric-covered structure that had as its basis a wooden box girder with ply-covered top and bottom and wire-braced sides; this was faired to a circular cross section by plywood formers and spruce stringers. A revised engine cowling

was fitted and the airscrew carried a small spinner. The fin and rudder were greatly enlarged, a constant-chord tailplane and elevators were fitted, and a separate tailskid, sprung and faired, was mounted on an extension of the rudder leading edge.

The interplane bracing was revised and augmented; and the reconstructed S.E.2 was one of the first aeroplanes to have streamline Rafwires in the interplane bracing in place of the stranded wire cables of the original aircraft. A twin-skid undercarriage was still fitted, but the skids were of modified shape.

The first recorded flight of the reconstructed S.E.2 was made on 3rd October 1914, with Frank Goodden at the controls. He and Geoffrey de Havilland shared the flying of the little single-seater while it was at Farnborough. It had the official serial number 609.

Later in 1914 the S.E.2 was sent to France,

and was allocated to No. 3 Squadron. It was given makeshift armament, originally consisting of two rifles firing at outward angles to clear the airscrew; later, only one 0.450 revolver was carried. J. T. B. McCudden noted that the S.E.2 was a little faster than the Bristol Scout B but had a slightly inferior climbing performance. It was certainly faster than any enemy type then in use, and if it had had worthwhile armament it might have been a useful fighter.

The S.E.2 was still with No.3 Squadron on 10th March 1915, but no longer figured anywhere in the R.F.C. Order of Battle two months later. There are indications in official papers that the aircraft may have been in existence when the war ended and that its preservation was sought. Unfortunately it did not survive, and its ultimate fate is unknown.

In later years the designation S.E.2a came to be applied to the reconstructed aircraft. Useful though the distinction provided by the suffix letter is, this designation was not used while the aircraft existed and cannot be regarded as authentic.

**Type:** *Single-seat scout.* **Power:** *80-h.p. Gnome seven-cylinder rotary engine.* **Armament:** *Originally two rifles, one on each side of the fuselage firing outwards to miss the airscrew; later one 0.450-in. calibre revolver.* **Performance:** *Maximum speed 96 m.p.h. at ground level.* **Weights:** *Loaded 1,200 lb.* **Dimensions:** *Span, 27 ft. 6¼ in.*

# S.E.4

Speaking in the discussion that followed a lecture delivered by Lt. Col. F. H. Sykes to the Royal Aeronautical Society on 4th February 1914, Brig. Gen. Sir David Henderson said, "If anyone wants to know which country has the fastest aeroplane in the world—it is Great

*The S.E.4 in its original form with tripod support for leaf-spring undercarriage axle.*

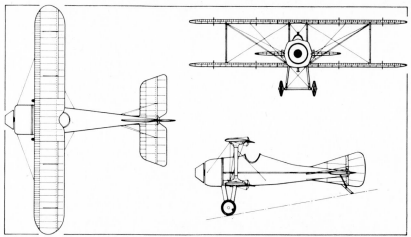

Britain". He was referring to the S.E.4, which had not flown at that date.

H. P. Folland had made some preliminary sketches for the S.E.3, which was designed with single I-struts between the mainplanes and trailing-edge flaps that could act as ailerons, be lowered to act as camber-changing flaps or be reflexed to reduce drag.

The S.E.3 was not built. It appears that it was abandoned in favour of the S.E.4, an advanced design in which everything possible was done to minimize drag. The engine, a 160-h.p. Gnome fourteen-cylinder rotary, was almost completely enclosed. The four-blade airscrew had a large spinner with a frontal opening; fan blades were fitted inside the spinner to assist in cooling the engine.

In construction the fuselage was more conventional than has been believed. Its basis was a full-length wooden box-girder, made in two parts that met just behind the cockpit; as on the S.E.2 the top and bottom of the rear portion were covered with plywood, the sides being cross-braced. The lower longitudinals of the forward portion were substantial *patons*, to which the spars of the lower centre section and the undercarriage were attached. Formers were fitted round the box girder to give an approximately circular cross section and the whole was covered with plywood. A transparent cockpit cover was designed and, after several attempts, successfully moulded in celluloid; but no-one could be induced to fly the S.E.4 with this in place and it was never used

The wings embodied the structure and

flaps intended for the S.E.3. Typical of the careful attention to detail was the use of special flush-fitting bolts to attach the sheet-steel end pieces to the shafts of the I-struts. The centre-section struts were hollow and concealed the upper aileron cables. The ailerons were full-span surfaces that could be reflexed or lowered in the same sense to act as camber-changing flaps. The tail surfaces were similar to those of the reconstructed S.E.2, and all gaps between flight controls and fixed surfaces were faired over with fine elastic netting.

When the S.E.4 emerged in June 1914 its undercarriage consisted of a tripod of struts to which was attached a spanwise leaf spring bearing a wheel at each end. With this undercarriage the S.E.4 rolled too much while taxying, so it was replaced in early August by a pair of conventional V-struts with a cross axle sprung by rubber cord.

The aircraft justified Brig. Gen. Henderson's boast of February 1914, for it had a maximum speed of 135 m.p.h. near the ground and an initial rate of climb of 1,600 ft./min.

Soon after the installation of the V-type undercarriage the S.E.4 was given an early camouflage paint scheme and the official serial number 628. It did not go to France, however, for it crashed at 11.45 a.m. on 12th

*The modified aircraft with V-strut undercarriage.*

August 1914 while being flown by Norman Spratt. It was reported that one of the wheels collapsed during a landing. The S.E.4 turned over and was so extensively damaged that it was abandoned.

Two designs for armoured single-seat scouts that would have borne some general resemblance to the S.E.4 were sketched out by H. P. Folland later in 1914 (the second is dated 28th December 1914). Neither was built, however, and there was no direct development from the S.E.4 design.

**Type:** *Single-seat scout.* **Power:** *160-h.p. Gnome fourteen-cylinder rotary engine.* **Armament:** *Nil.* **Performance:** *Maximum speed 135 m.p.h. at ground level; initial rate of climb, over 1,600 ft. per min.; endurance 1 hour.* **Weights:** *No details available.* **Dimensions:** *Span, 27 ft. 6¼ in.; length, 21 ft. 4 in.; height, 8 ft. 11⅞ in. with tripod undercarriage, 9 ft. 10½ in. with V-type undercarriage; wing area 198 sq. ft.*

## S.E.4a

Despite its designation, the S.E.4a owed virtually nothing to the S.E.4. It had full-span control surfaces on the wings and the first of the four aircraft built had a large spinner with an internal cooling fan, but beyond that the S.E.4a had nothing in common with its

*The first S.E.4a, with large spinner and fully faired fuselage, at Farnborough, 25th June 1915.*

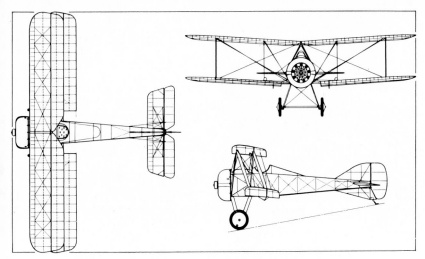

predecessor. It had been designed as an aircraft that could be used for the purpose of obtaining information on stability and manoeuvrability and might also be suitable for operational use. Its design incorporated all the experience the Royal Aircraft Factory had acquired in the development of such stable aircraft as the R.E.1 and B.E.2c.

From the operational standpoint the S.E.4a would have been a more practical aircraft than the highly refined S.E.4. It was a neat and sturdy little single-bay biplane with pronounced stagger. The upper wings met at a trestle-shaped cabane structure; the lower mainplanes were attached to two spanwise steel-tube members. The fuselage was made in two parts: the forward portion was of steel tubing; the rear was a wooden box-girder with plywood webs top and bottom and cross-braced sides. Armour was provided to protect the pilot. The tailplane and elevators were similar to those of the S.E.4, and the general appearance and disposition of the vertical surfaces foreshadowed the S.E.5.

The first S.E.4a, which underwent its pre-flight inspection on 23rd June 1915, embodied several refinements. Apart from its spinner, already mentioned, it had faired fuselage sides and stub-wing fairings over the steel-tube members connecting the lower wings; the aileron cables were led through the lower wing and the pulleys were fitted inside the

*The third S.E.4a typified all the subsequent aircraft of the type, having a flat-sided fuselage, smaller head fairing and no spinner. When this photograph was taken, on 29th July 1915, the aircraft had the 80-h.p. Le Rhône engine.*

wing, and the headrest was faired into the fuselage. The engine was an 80-h.p. Gnome. The other S.E.4a's had no spinner, flat-sided fuselages with smaller headrests, and external aileron pulleys and cables.

On 25th June 1915 the first S.E.4a made its first flight in the hands of Frank Goodden. It was flown at Farnborough on various dates by Goodden and W. Stutt until 13th August, after which it disappears from the record.

The second machine, which was also powered by the 80-h.p. Gnome, was passed for flight on 16th July 1915 and made its first flight five days later. It visited Upavon on 9th August and was last mentioned in the Farnborough records on 20th August.

This S.E.4a was closely followed by the other two. The third aircraft was approved on 25th July 1915, and was flown for the first time two days later by Stutt. It was originally fitted with an 80-h.p. Le Rhône engine, but this had been replaced by an 80-h.p. Gnome by the beginning of September 1915. The fourth S.E.4a had been completed by 9th August, was passed for flight on the 11th, and made its first flight on the 13th. Two of the S.E.4a's are known to have had the official serial numbers 5609 and 5611.

The relatively low power of the S.E.4a prevented it from approaching the spectacular performance of the S.E.4 but it was manoeuvrable. Frank Goodden found it an excellent aerobatic aircraft; although his displays delighted his colleagues that was not their primary purpose, and his observations and reports provided valuable data that were used to great advantage in later designs.

It is believed that at least two S.E.4a's went to Home Defence units. One was stationed at Hounslow but was wrecked on 24th September 1915; it had spun in while being flown by Captain B. Blood. In the following months another S.E.4a was stationed at Joyce Green as an anti-Zeppelin aircraft but was apparently never in action.

Details of the armament of these S.E.4a's have not been discovered. Only the first machine is known to have had a gun mounting of any kind while it was at Farnborough: there were brackets for a single gun above the cabane.

The third S.E.4a apparently stayed at Farnborough, where it was flown a great deal.

Among its distinguished pilots were Lieutenant Frank Courtney, Captain Roderic Hill and Dr. F. A. Lindemann (later Lord Cherwell); and it was fitted with an 80 h.p. Clerget engine in October 1916, but it is not known whether it retained this engine thereafter. It continued to be flown at least until 5th September 1917, when it concluded a series of accelerometer test flights that had begun in August.

**Type:** *Single-seat scout.* **Power:** *80-h.p. Gnome; 80-h.p. Le Rhône; 80-h.p. Clerget.* **Armament:** *A single gun could be carried above the upper wing.* **Performance:** *No details available.* **Weights:** *No details available.* **Dimensions:** *Span, 27 ft. 5.2 in.; length, 20 ft. 11½ in.; height, 9 ft. 5 in.*

# S.E.5

In the summer of 1915 Lt-Col. H. R. M. Brooke-Popham, then G.S.O.1 at Royal Flying Corps Headquarters, inspected an early example of the 150-h.p. Hispano-Suiza engine in Paris. On his recommendation the first British order for the Hispano-Suiza was placed in August 1915; negotiations for the manufacture of the engine in England were subsequently started. A faster-running geared version of the engine, giving just over 200 h.p. at 2,000 r.p.m., followed the original 150-h.p. direct-drive type.

The Royal Aircraft Factory designed two single-seat fighters round the Hispano-Suiza. The first of these was a compact tractor biplane for which the designed armament was a single Lewis machine-gun mounted on the centre line and firing between the two banks of cylinders: a geared form of the engine was envisaged, its hollow airscrew shaft being at the necessary height to permit the bullets to pass through it. This type was designated S.E.5. The other design was the F.E.10, similar in configuration to the freakish B.E.9, with a 150-h.p. Hispano-Suiza.

Fortunately good sense prevailed and the S.E.5 design was chosen for development, the main design work being done by J. Kenworthy and H. P. Folland. The first of three prototypes, A4561, was submitted for its final inspection at noon on 20th November 1916. It differed in certain respects from the first drawings of June 1916 but was substantially similar to the preliminary layout. It was unarmed, and was powered by a 150-h.p. direct-drive engine (No. H.5213/W.D.10100) made at the Hispano-Suiza company's Paris factory. The gravity tank was fitted inside the leading-edge portion of the port upper wing, and small windows let into the sides of the top decking beside the rear centre-section struts suggest that the original idea of fitting a

*The first prototype S.E.5 in its original form at Farnborough, 23rd November 1916, with gravity tank in the leading edge of the port upper wing.*

single central Lewis gun might not have been completely abandoned. With the direct-drive engine no such form of armament was possible, of course. The first recorded flight of A4561 was made at 10 a.m. on 22nd November 1916; the pilot was Major F. W. Goodden. On the following day it was flown by Captain Albert Ball.

On 27th November the second prototype, A4562, began its final inspection, which was completed on 1st December 1916. Its first recorded flight was made three days later; again Frank Goodden was at the controls. This S.E.5 was virtually identical with A4561, having a 150-h.p. Hispano-Suiza engine (No. 5193/W.D. 10104) driving a two-blade airscrew.

The second S.E.5 was damaged a few days

after its first flight. By 21st December it had been fitted with a new landing gear and full armament: one Vickers gun in the fuselage, offset to port, and a Lewis gun on a Foster mounting above the centre section. A new and greatly enlarged windscreen that enclosed the breech of the Vickers gun was fitted and there were no windows in the decking forward of the cockpit. The aircraft had a new gravity tank mounted externally above the centre section, and there was a wind-driven fuel pump under the fuselage. Goodden flew A4562 to St. Omer on 24th December, possibly to demonstrate the new fighter to operational pilots. The aircraft's recorded flights there were curiously few, but it underwent some detail modifications and was flown back to Farnborough by Lt. F. H. B. Selous on 4th January 1917.

The third prototype, A4563, was submitted for final inspection on 12th January 1917. It was powered by a 200-h.p. geared Hispano-Suiza driving a large-diameter left-hand air-screw, and its radiator differed slightly from those of its predecessors. The gravity petrol tank was, as on A4562, mounted externally above the centre section. This was in fact a double tank, one part of which contained pet-rol, the other water for the radiator. Otherwise, A4563 was very similar to A4561, even to the small windows in the sides of the decking ahead of the cockpit.

As A4563 had been fitted with the centre section and port upper wing of A4561 the structure of these surfaces had to be modified. A4561 itself had been fitted with a new centre section with an enlarged trailing-edge cut-out and the overwing gravity tank. This first prototype was by this time also fitted with a Vickers gun and side extensions of its wind-screen.

Having passed its pre-flight inspection on 12th January the third S.E.5, A4563, was flown for the first time later that day by Frank Gooden. Following the loss of A4562 described in the following paragraph, this third prototype was quite extensively modified and, with armament fitted, became in effect the prototype S.E.5a, the history of which is related separately in pages 82–91.

The development flying of the S.E.5 cost the

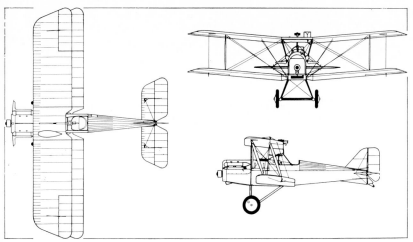

life of Major Goodden, who was then one of Britain's finest test pilots. On 28th January 1917 he was flying A4562 at Farnborough when it broke up in the air and he was killed. Investigation by the late Dr. A. P. Thurston showed that, contrary to the opinion of the official committee of enquiry, the wings had failed in downward torsion. In support of his views he was able to show indications of incipient failure in the wings of one of the other prototypes. Plywood webs added to the compression ribs cured the trouble and were standardized for all later S.E.5s and 5a's. The collapse of A4562's wing structure was helped by unsatisfactory strut-to-spar connexions, which had enabled the interplane struts to come out. Improved fittings were designed for the production aircraft.

All the production S.E.5s were built at the Royal Aircraft Factory. The first, A4845,

*This photograph is believed to be the first ever published of the second prototype, A4562. It was taken after the installation of the aircraft's armament and shows that A4562 had a large windscreen somewhat similar to the "greenhouse" fitted to the production S.E.5. In the cockpit is Major Frank Goodden, who was killed while flying this prototype on 28th January 1917.*

*The third prototype, A4563, in its original form without armament, 15th January 1917. At this time the aircraft was very similar to A4561 but had the 200-h.p. Hispano-Suiza engine.*

passed inspection on 2nd March 1917, and was followed during that month by A4846–A4868. All these aircraft as originally built had wings of the same planform as those of the prototypes with widely raked tips. Martlesham was severely critical of the lateral control, especially at low air speeds, and reported that A4845 "was almost uncontrollable below 70 m.p.h. in gusts." This was improved by reducing the angle of rake of the wing tips, a modification that took 1 ft. 3.6 in. off the overall span.

The early production S.E.5s dispensed with the armoured seat that had been fitted to the prototype, but had an even larger windscreen than that of A4562. This was a cumbersome, asymmetrical affair that was taken farther aft than on A4562 and interfered with the pilot's forward view. No. 56 Squadron was the first R.F.C. unit to receive the S.E.5, and its pilots unanimously condemned this "greenhouse". At least two aircraft, A4850 and A4853, were modified by the squadron before it left England. Both aircraft had been fitted with a

small plain Avro-type windscreen by 7th April 1917; the forward top-decking of A4853 had been modified to enclose the breech of the Vickers gun and a fabric-covered head fairing fitted.

A4850 was Ball's S.E.5 and was more extensively modified. An Avro-type windscreen and a smaller, plywood-covered head fairing were fitted; the Vickers gun was removed and replaced by a second Lewis gun firing at a downward angle through the bottom of the fuselage; a new centre-section with built-in gravity tank and water header tank and an enlarged trailing-edge cut-out was apparently specially made for this S.E.5. After No. 56 Squadron reached France Ball dispensed with the downward-firing Lewis, installed a Vickers gun externally above the fuselage, and fitted Spad-type exhaust pipes in place of the L-shaped manifolds of the early production S.E.5.

Major Blomfield, the officer commanding No. 56 Squadron, kept his unit out of opera-

*Typical production S.E.5 with modified wing tips, large windscreen and overwing gravity tank, Farnborough, 1st May 1917. A few days later A8904 was in operational use with No. 56 Squadron, R.F.C.*

tions until all aircraft had been fitted with the small windscreen. Thus, although the squadron had gone to France on 8th April it did not fly its first offensive patrol until 22nd April. At first Ball did not like the S.E. but quickly came to appreciate its strength, speed and fire

power. In combat it soon proved itself to be a considerable weapon.

Aircraft of the second production batch (starting at A8898) were delivered during the second half of April 1917. These S.E.5s were built with the short-span wings, and the first

*Captain Albert Ball in his modified S.E.5 A4850 at London Colney, late March 1917.*

aircraft of the batch (to A8917 at least) had the large windscreen and overwing gravity tank. Movable shutters were fitted to the upper half of the radiator. A8917 itself was completed without armament, but had the gravity and water tanks in the leading edge of the centre section. Later aircraft in this batch were delivered with the 200-h.p. Hispano-Suiza.

At most, 59 S.E.5s were built. Most were used by No. 56 Squadron, but some went to No. 60, a few to Nos. 24 and 85 Squadrons. The type was replaced by the S.E.5a as soon as supplies of the 200-h.p. engine permitted.

**Type:** *Single-seat fighter.* **Power:** *One 150-h.p. Hispano-Suiza eight-cylinder water-cooled engine.* **Armament:** *One fixed, synchronized*

*Production S.E.5 A8898 in the field, wearing the markings used by No. 60 Squadron for a short time in 1917.*

81

0.303-in. Vickers machine-gun; one 0.303-in. Lewis machine-gun on Foster mounting. **Performance:** *Maximum speed 122 m.p.h. at 3,000 ft., 119 m.p.h. at 6,500 ft., 114 m.p.h. at 10,000 ft., 98 m.p.h. at 15,000 ft., climb to 6,500 ft., 8 min.; to 10,000 ft., 14 min. 15 sec.; ceiling 19,000 ft.; endurance 2½ hours.* **Weights:** *Empty 1,399 lb., loaded 1,935 lb.* **Dimensions:** *Span, 27 ft. 11 in., later 26 ft. 7½ in.; length, 20 ft. 11 in.; height 9 ft. 5 in.; wing area, 249.8 sq. ft., later 244 sq. ft.*

## S.E.5a

On 29th May 1917 Captain Roderic Hill flew the third prototype S.E.5, A4563, from Farnborough to Martlesham Heath. The original form of this aircraft is described in the history of the S.E.5 on page 77. When A4563 went to Martlesham, however, it had a

*The modified third prototype, A4563, in the form in which it was tested at Martlesham Heath in May 1917, with full armament, four-blade airscrew and L-shaped exhaust manifolds.*

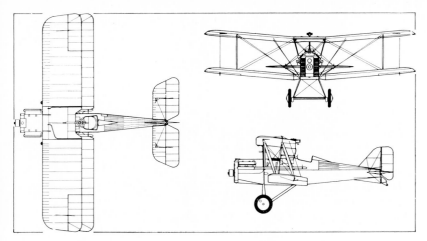

200-h.p. Hispano-Suiza engine driving a four-blade airscrew and the gravity petrol and water tanks were in the centre-section leading-edge. A head fairing was fitted behind the cockpit, and the aircraft had the short-span wings.

The performance of this 200 h.p. S.E. was substantially better than that of the 150-h.p. S.E.5. The design was therefore standardized for large scale production, more or less in the final form of A4563, as the S.E.5a. Contracts had been given as early as February 1917 to Martinsyde Ltd. (for B1-B200) and Vickers Ltd. (for B501–B700). The Royal Aircraft Factory fitted the 200-h.p. Hispano-Suiza to at least fifteen aircraft of the batch A8898–A8947; the first of these was A8923 which had been completed as early as 30th May and was therefore virtually contem-porary with the prototype. Several of these early S.E.5a's had Wolseley-built 200-h.p. Hispano-Suiza engines, in spite of the troubles that had been experienced with the Wolseley Hispanos and, at that early date, can hardly have been overcome. The first few aircraft, like A4563, retained the L-shaped exhaust manifolds of the S.E.5; later S.E.5a's had the characteristic long horizontal pipes. All S.E.5a's had the modified wings of reduced span.

Some of the early S.E.5a's were delivered to No. 56 Squadron, which received its first example of the type in June 1917 and pro-gressively replaced its S.E.5s with S.E.5a's. In this squadron the long exhaust pipes were cut off and replaced by short extensions of the manifold. In July 1917 Vickers-built S.E.5a's began to come forward, and deliveries of

Martinsyde-built aircraft of the batch B1–B200 also started. Additional contracts were given to several other manufacturers in 1917; during that year no fewer than 3,600 S.E.5a's were ordered, the last contracts for the year being dated 29th December. By the end of 1917 appreciably more than 800 S.E.5s and 5a's had been built. Yet only 335 had gone to R.F.C. squadrons in France and 105 to training units; and of the total of 440 about 60 were S.E.5s. At the front, only Nos. 41, 40, 56, 60 and 84 Squadrons of the R.F.C. were operational with the S.E.5a; during December No. 68 Squadron was re-equipped with the type, and No. 24 Squadron started to do so. In January 1918 the balance of some 400 S.E.5a's were held in store: no engines were available for them.

Formidable difficulties beset the production programme for the 200-h.p. Hispano-Suiza engine. In the United Kingdom only Wolseley Motors Ltd. held a licence to manufacture it, and their early 200-h.p. engines had proved to be seriously defective. Some S.E.5a's had French-made Hispano-Suiza engines, but in those manufactured by the Brasier company the reduction gears and airscrew shaft had to be replaced by British-made spares. Ultimately by October 1917, the engine-supply difficulty assumed crisis proportions and these faulty engines had to be passed into service with defective gears. Relief came in January 1918 in the form of deliveries of the first of 8,000 Hispano-Suiza engines that the Air Board had, at the insistence of the Admiralty, ordered from other French manufacturers at the end of 1916.

The troubles of the Wolseley engines had manifested themselves in May 1917. As a precaution against complete failure of the 200-h.p. engine the firm were asked to produce an additional 400 engines of the original 150-h.p. direct-drive type. The instructions given to Wolseley were not clear enough, and the company developed the engine into a high-compression power unit that was designated

Wolseley W.4A Viper; its normal output at ground level was 220 h.p. at 2,000 r.p.m.

This development work naturally delayed Wolseley production: whereas it had been intended that 140 engines should be delivered by the end of August 1917 only ten Vipers had been made. One was fitted to the S.E.5a B4862; after inspection on 24th August the aircraft went to Martlesham Heath for official trials on the following day. This aircraft had a single radiator with rounded top, and the complete installation did not differ materially from that of the 200-h.p. Hispano-Suiza.

Martlesham flew B4862 with its engine's compression ratio at its original value of 5.68 and subsequently at 5.3. Overall, the 5.3 compression pistons gave slightly better results and were standardized. A second Viper installation was made in B4899 (which had exchanged identities with B4891 in mid-November) at the end of 1917. These Viper-powered S.E.5a's were subjected to official performance tests in September and December 1917 respectively. Performance was rather better than with the Wolseley-built 200-h.p. geared engine, and the Viper itself was

*Standard production S.E.5a, B4867, with French-made Hispano-Suiza engine driving a four-blade airscrew and fitted with long exhaust pipes.*

(*Left*) *Of the few S.E.5a's that were fitted with narrow-chord elevators, B4890 was captured intact by the Germans. It is seen here in German hands after being forced down by aircraft of* Jagdstaffel 5.

(*Right*) *A Home Defence S.E.5a of No. 50 Squadron with flame dampers fitted to the ends of the exhaust pipes. In the cockpit is Captain G. S. M. Insall, V.C.*

*Late-production S.E.5a with standard Wolseley Viper installation and wooden undercarriage V-struts.*

regarded as satisfactory.

Another alternative to the 200-h.p. Hispano-Suiza was tried in the S.E.5a. On 13th November 1917 B4900 was submitted for final inspection at the R.A.F. Farnborough with a 200-h.p. Sunbeam Arab I engine; it appears that this aircraft had two radiator blocks in place of the single-unit radiator fitted to the 200-h.p. Hispano-Suiza engine. At least five other S.E.5a's were fitted with the Arab engine at Farnborough, one (C1111) having both the Arab I (geared) and Arab II (direct-drive). In February 1918 an S.E.5a was fitted with an Arab II at Martlesham, originally with an underslung radiator. Farnborough persevered with the Arab until the spring of 1919, but the engine was basically unsatisfactory and was dogged by serious vibration troubles. It was not adopted as a standard power unit for the S.E.5a.

The Viper was specified for all S.E.5a's ordered under 1918 contracts. Many did in fact have that engine, and the production aircraft had twin radiator blocks in an installation of more angular appearance than that of the 200-h.p. Hispano-Suiza. Those S.E.5a's that did not have Vipers were delivered with such engines as were available. From France 2,292 Hispano-Suizas of the 200-h.p. type were delivered to the British flying services in the first six months of 1918. These came from various manufacturers, the later engines having the compression ratio increased to 5.3:1; this raised the power output to 220-h.p. at the

*The S.E.5a with the experimental Viper installation that had an underslung radiator.*

normal engine speed of 2,000 r.p.m. All earlier 200-h.p. engines were fitted with the high-compression pistons when overhauled.

In 1918 the S.E.5a built up a formidable reputation as a fighting aircraft. Although it did not have the Camel's lightning-swift response to the controls, it combined manoeuvrability with strength, stability and (by the standards of the period) comfort. By the time of the Armistice the S.E.5a equipped fourteen British, one Australian and two American squadrons on the Western Front, and it was in use with two squadrons in Palestine, one in Mesopotamia and three in

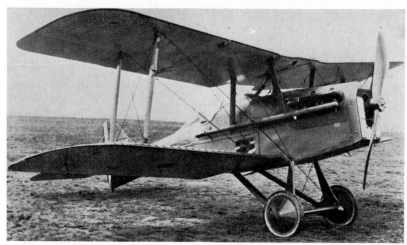

*B4875 with Eeman gun mounting carrying three Lewis guns firing upwards at an angle of 45 deg., November 1917.*

*The extensively modified D203 at Farnborough, 29th August 1918. This S.E.5a had a modified fin and rudder, Viper radiators for its geared 200-h.p. Hispano-Suiza, and narrow-chord ailerons; its mainplanes were rigged without dihedral.*

Macedonia. It had been tried by fourteen Home Defence squadrons, but its water-cooled engine took longer to warm up than did the Camel's rotary, and the S.E.5a's pilot's view for landing at night was less satisfactory, consequently it was withdrawn.

The S.E.5a was well able to hold its own in combat right up to the time of Armistice but the design continued to be refined. Towards the end of 1917 a stronger undercarriage was standardized. This had wooden struts, the forward leg on each side being a substantial tapered strut. Other modifications to the structure were less discernible: improved oil tanks, strengthened trailing edges, revised fin structure; all were introduced.

In service, pilots made modifications of their own. Many preferred to remove the head fairing from behind the cockpit in order to improve the rearward view; most squadrons thought it advisable to fit an additional bracing wire to the leading edge of the fin. It has been reported that No. 41 Squadron tried to install twin Vickers guns on their S.E.5a's, but this form of armament was not standardized.

Earlier attempts had been made at Farnborough to improve on the aircraft's armament. In September 1917 B4885 was fitted with twin Lewis guns in addition to the usual Vickers; this was probably done to try out an idea submitted by No. 56 Squadron. At that time, however, the centre-section was regarded as insufficiently strong even for the standard single Lewis gun (it was subsequently strengthened) and the twin-Lewis arrangement came to naught.

A different triple-gun installation was made in B4875 in November 1917. This aircraft had an Eeman mounting in the fuselage, carrying three Lewis guns firing forwards and upwards at 45° through slots in the centre section. Apparently a Home Defence application was envisaged, but the installation was not operationally practical and it was not pursued.

Farnborough conducted many experiments with modified wing and control surfaces including twin fins and rudders. Ailerons and elevators of reduced chord were fitted, and similar modifications were made to some operational S.E.5a's. Narrow-chord elevators were fitted to B4890, and McCudden recorded that B4891 also had narrow-chord elevators when he took it over on 3rd December 1917.

An experimental installation of a Viper with

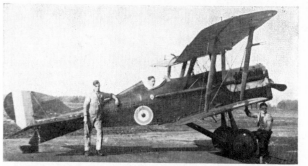

*Another S.E.5a with a modified tail unit was E5923, seen here at Martlesham Heath in 1920. In addition to its Pfalz-like fin and rudder it had a triangular two-piece tailplane of which the rear section was adjustable and inversely tapered elevators.*

an underslung radiator was tested in March 1918. It is believed that this was thought likely to make the S.E.5a more suitable for service in Mesopotamia, but the speed at 15,000 ft. was reduced by 14½ m.p.h. and the climb to that height took five minutes longer than with the standard Viper, consequently this idea was abandoned for the standard S.E.5a.

Of far greater significance was the testing, in September 1918, of the Hart variable-pitch

*The only all-American S.E.5a was S.C.43153.*

airscrew in C1134. This was unsuccessful, and the S.E. was fitted with a standard airscrew in October. The R.A.E. pursued the development of v.p. airscrews, however, and C1148 and C1091 were fitted with other types after the Armistice.

During 1918 extensive experiments with parachutes were conducted with several operational types of aircraft. One of these was the S.E.5a, on which the Mears parachute and

the Calthrop Guardian Angel A.1 were tested. Several S.E.5a's were used, and at least five different methods of stowing the parachute were tried.

In the U.S.A. the Curtiss company assembled fifty-six S.E.5a's from British-made components and was given a contract for 1,000 S.E.5a's for the U.S. Air Service. The Curtiss-built aircraft were to have the 180-h.p. Wright-Martin Hispano-Suiza engine. Only one, S.C.43153, was completed, however; the balance of the order was cancelled at the Armistice.

The war over, the S.E.5a disappeared rapidly. The type remained in service in small numbers in Australia, Canada and South Africa; in the U.S.A. the Eberhardt company modified a number of aircraft for post-war service under the designation S.E.5E. In the United Kingdom a few specimens survived for some years, mostly as experimental aircraft at the R.A.E. Farnborough; others assumed civil identities, and some pioneered sky-writing.

**Type:** *Single-seat fighter.* **Power:** *One 200-h.p. Hispano-Suiza; 220-h.p. Hispano-Suiza; 200-h.p. Wolseley W.4A Viper; 200-h.p. Wolseley Adder; 200-h.p. Sunbeam Arab. All were water-cooled eight-cylinder engines.* **Armament:** *One fixed, synchronized 0.303-in. Vickers machine-gun; one 0.303-in. Lewis machine-gun on Foster mounting; four 25-lb Cooper bombs.* **Performance** *(200-h.p. Hispano-Suiza): Maximum speed 126 m.p.h. at 10,000 ft., 116.5 m.p.h. at 15,000 ft.; climb to 10,000 ft., 13 min. 15 sec.; to 15,000 ft., 27 min. 35 sec.; service ceiling 17,000 ft.; endurance 2¼ hours.* **Weights** *(200-h.p. Hispano-Suiza): Empty 1,531 lb., loaded 2,048 lb.* **Dimensions:** *Span, 26 ft. 7.4 in.; length, 20 ft. 11 in.; height, 9ft. 6 in.; wing area, 245.8 sq. ft.*

## S.E.5b

The S.E.5a A8947 was completed at the end of June 1917 as a standard aircraft powered by an Aries-built 200-h.p. Hispano-Suiza No. 10317/W.D.10171 and armed with Vickers gun No. C2738 and Lewis gun No. 33699. It was submitted for its final pre-flight inspection on 29th June and had been cleared by 8.30 a.m. on the following day.

Early in 1918 it was extensively modified, and on 4th April it was again submitted for inspection with the new designation S.E.5b. In this form it had new wings of unequal span and chord: the dimensions of the upper wing were respectively 30 ft. 7 in. and 6 ft.; those of the lower were 26 ft. 6 in. and 4 ft. 3 in. These corresponded with 26 ft. 7.4 in. and 5 ft. on the standard S.E.5a. On the S.E.5b the interplane struts had a pronounced outward rake, and the upper ailerons were hinged to an auxiliary spar a short distance aft of the rear main spar.

*The S.E.5b A8947 at Farnborough on 30th April 1918.*

A considerable refinement of the lines of the forward fuselage was made possible by the use of a retractable underslung radiator that could be swung back into the fuselage. A large shallow spinner was fitted to the airscrew and

91

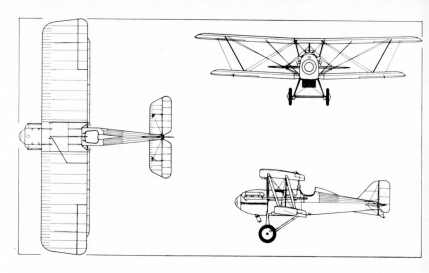

a cowling of good streamline form was fitted about the engine. The S.E.5b retained its original engine, which had had its reduction gearing removed and drove a right-hand Etoile airscrew.

It was hoped that the sesquiplane wings would improve the rate of climb and give the pilot a better all-round view than he had on the S.E.5a, and that the cleaner nose would enhance performance generally. The results were not wholly beneficial, for the greater drag of the larger upper wing cancelled out any benefit that was derived from the faired nose.

No attempt seems to have been made to develop the S.E.5b as a replacement for the S.E.5a. By 9th January 1919 it had been fitted with a set of standard S.E.5a wings and was subsequently flown at the R.A.E. in a series of comparative trials with a standard S.E.5a and with E5923, an S.E.5a that had been fitted with an extensively modified tail unit (see p. 90) at Martlesham Heath. In the course of a series of handling experiments the S.E.5b was fitted with a horizontal tail of the same total area as that of the S.E.5a but with the elevator area reduced from 50% to 35% of the total. The S.E.5b was regarded as being the best of the three aircraft.

Later experiments compared the effectiveness of the S.E.5b's underslung radiator with

*Side view, also dated 30th April 1918, illustrates the unequal chord of upper and lower wings.*

the frontal radiator of the S.E.5a. As might be expected, these showed that the S.E.5a radiator was the better in normal flight, but when gliding with radiator retracted the S.E.5b had a better gliding angle.

It seems that the S.E.5b did not revert to its sesquiplane wings, but it remained in service at the R.A.E. for some years after the Armistice. It was flown at the first R.A.F. Pageant at Hendon in July 1920, when Flt.-Lt. J. Noakes gave a spectacular display of aerobatics.

**Type:** *Single-seat fighter.* **Power:** *One 200-h.p. Hispano-Suiza eight-cylinder water-cooled engine.* **Armament:** *One fixed, synchronized 0.303-in. Vickers machine-gun; one 0.303-in. Lewis machine-gun on Foster mounting.* **Performance:** *No details available.* **Weights:** *Loaded* 1,950 *lb.* **Dimensions:** *Span, upper* 30 *ft.* 7 *in., lower* 26 *ft.* 6 *in.; length,* 20 *ft.* 10 *in.; height,* 9 *ft.* 6 *in.; wing area,* 278 *sq. ft.*

*The S.E.5b with standard S.E.5a wings.*

## SAGE TYPE 2

Another of the many firms to become Admiralty contractors for the manufacture of aircraft was the Peterborough firm of shop-fitters, Frederick Sage & Co., Ltd. Their wood-working shops began building Short 184 sea-planes in 1915 and early in the following year the firm set up their own design office under E. C. Gordon England.

The first Sage design was not built; it was for a twin-engine bomber. Their Type 2 was designed by Clifford W. Tinson, who had begun his design career as Frank Barnwell's assistant on the Bristol Scout. The Sage Type 2 was intended to be a fighting aircraft, and, at a time when no machine-gun synchronizing gear was available to British designers, repre-sented yet another method of fitting a tractor biplane with a machine gun that could be used reasonably effectively.

It was a two-seater, but was rather smaller than contemporary single-seaters. The crew sat in a fully-glazed cabin that supported the upper wing; a hole was cut in the wing above the observer's seat, and by standing up he could wield the Lewis gun that constituted the Sage scout's armament and had a clear field of fire in all upward and most rearward directions. The lower wing was of much smaller chord

94

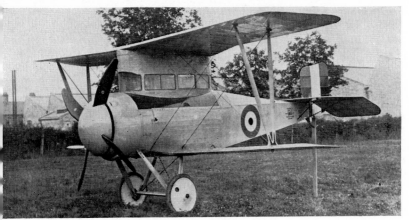

(*Above*) *The Sage Type 2 photographed at the Peterborough factory of Frederick Sage & Co., Ltd.*

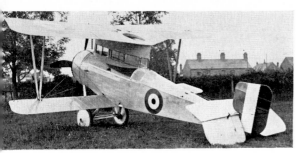

(*Left*) *To fire his Lewis gun, the observer of the Sage Type 2 had to stand up with his head and shoulders through the cut-out in the upper wing.*

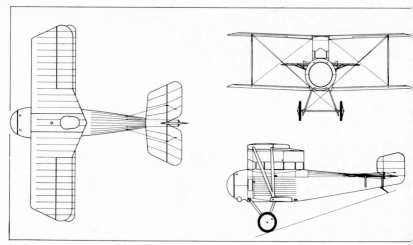

than the upper and had only one main spar; V-type interplane struts were fitted. Ailerons were fitted to the upper wings only.

Structurally the Sage Type 2 was conventional. Care had been taken to reduce drag: the 100-h.p. Gnome Monosoupape rotary engine was fully cowled, and the four-blade airscrew had a large spinner. A hint of Bristol Scout influence was present in the shape of the balanced rudder, but in every major aspect the Sage 2 was a good example of compact, neat design.

Its career was brief: it flew for the first time on 10th August 1916 and crashed at Cranwell on 20th September 1916 when the rudder post collapsed. Although the Sage 2 had proved to have a remarkably good performance and to

be manoeuvrable, no attempt was made to re build or develop it. Gun-synchronizing gear had been developed while the Sage 2 was bein, built, and the better-armed Sopwith 1½ Strutter was already in squadron service.

**Type:** *Two-seat fighting scout.* **Power:** *One* 100 *h.p. Gnome Monosoupape nine-cylinder rotary engine.* **Armament:** *One 0.303-in. Lewis machine gun.* **Performance:** *112 m.p.h. at ground level 109.75 m.p.h. at 10,000 ft., 104 m.p.h. a 15,000 ft.; climb to 10,000 ft., 14 min. 45 sec. to 15,000 ft., 35 min.; ceiling 16,000 ft.; en durance 2½ hours.* **Weights:** *Empty 890 lb. loaded 1,546 lb.* **Dimensions:** *Span, 22 ft. 2½ in.; length, 21 ft. 1⅝ in.; height, 9 ft. 6 in.; wing area, 168 sq. ft.*

# SIDDELEY S.R.2 SISKIN

During the first world war the Royal Aircraft Factory was the object of a great deal of criticism, much of it vindictive, ill-informed and inaccurate. A great deal of good work was done there, not least in the field of aero-engine design; the fundamental work on air-cooled engines that was done by the late Professor A. H. Gibson at Farnborough in 1915–16 made possible whole generations of aircraft power units.

In September 1916 the Royal Aircraft Factory designed the 300-h.p. R.A.F.8 engine, a 14-cylinder two-row radial engine with a dis-

placement of 1,374 cu. in.; an advanced feature of the engine was an integral gear-driven super-charger designed by J. E. Ellor. Owing to the implementation of the recommendations of the Burbidge Report the R.A.F.8 was never built at Farnborough. In January 1917 Captain F. M. Green relinquished his post as Chief Engineer at the Royal Aircraft Factory and became chief aeronautical engineer of the Siddeley-Deasy Motor Car Co., Ltd., of Coventry. His primary task was the development of the Siddeley Puma engine, but he was granted permission to develop the R.A.F.8

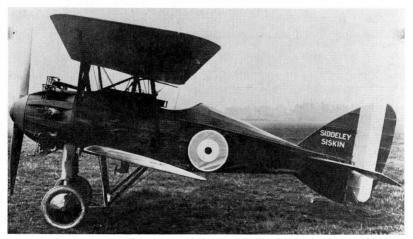

*Siskin photographed at its maker's works.*

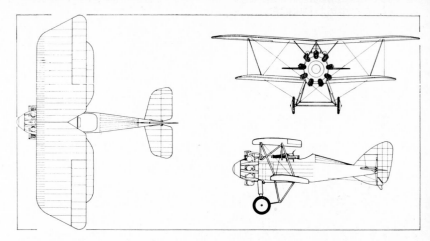

engine. The necessary design work was done by the late S. D. Heron and the engine was named Siddeley Jaguar.

Just before Captain Green had left the Royal Aircraft Factory the design of the S.E.6 had been prepared. This was an equal-span biplane with N-type interplane bracing and a fin and rudder of characteristic shape, powered by a 200-h.p. R.A.F.4d engine. Green also sketched out a rough preliminary layout for the S.E.7. Its precise configuration is not known, but it was intended to have the R.A.F.8 engine and incorporated a fin and rudder similar in shape to those of the projected S.E.6. A wind-tunnel model of a fuselage that may have been considered for the S.E.7 had a radial engine in a complete cowling, several feet in chord, that gave the fuselage remarkably clean lines.

It seems likely that Captain Green used his preliminary ideas for the S.E.7 as the basis of the first single-seat fighter to be built by the Siddeley-Deasy company. Unfortunately, the date of design is not known, but it seems likely that the Siddeley fighter preceded such types as the Nighthawk, Ara and Basilisk. Certainly the official contract for prototypes was given at a time when it was still the practice to allot serial numbers for six aircraft.

The firm's type number S.R.2 was applied to the aircraft. An official report dated 26th June 1918 states that the first S.R.2, C4541, was at that time "being erected". This suggests that all major structural work was completed, whereas the same report indicates that the Nighthawk, Snark, Snapper, Basilisk and Ara were then only partially built. All these types

are mentioned by name as single-seat fighters (high altitude) powered by the 320-h.p. A.B.C. Dragonfly engine and falling under R.A.F. Type I; but the S.R.2, unnamed at that time, was listed among "Experimental machines possessing features likely to be of use to the Air Force" and its engine appears merely as a "300-h.p. radial".

From all this it would not be unreasonable to assume that the Siddeley S.R.2 was in fact the S.E.7 design, worked out in detail but still, even at that date, intended to have the R.A.F.8 engine.

About the middle of 1918 the contract for S.R.2s was reduced to three prototypes and the Dragonfly engine was specified for the type. By the end of July the bare airframe had been erected and controls, tanks and guns were being fitted. Work on C4542 and C4543 had begun; the former was ready for its engine by mid-September but apparently no Dragonfly was available for it or for C4541. The A.I.D. were satisfied with the aircraft's strength but warned that the widely raked upper wing tips were very flexible and would have to be watched.

With the adoption of the Nighthawk the S.R.2, in common with its competitors, had to wait until December 1918, when one Dragonfly engine was given to each manufacturer having a prototype embodying the power unit. The aircraft itself had been officially named Siskin.

The first Siskin was flying in April 1919. It was a compact single-bay sesquiplane, distinguished by an unusual form of undercarriage and a remarkably clean installation of its Dragonfly engine. There was no upper centre section: the two halves of the upper wing met at the centre line and were supported by two W-form systems of struts. As the upper mainplane was almost level with the pilot's eyes it interfered little with his field of view, and each half wing tapered in thickness for a short distance towards the root.

It seems that the Siskin was regarded as a promising type, for Dragonfly engines were provided for C4542 and C4543, and the latter is reported to have gone to Martlesham in July 1919 for trials that were concluded in September. Martlesham also tested C4541, and recorded good performance figures for the

*C4541 with an early Armstrong Siddeley Jaguar engine and horn-balanced rudder.*

type. Most remarkable of all is a report that, in 1919, work on C4544 and C4545 had begun, indicating that the contract had again been amended to revert to its original size. What is not known is the precise configuration of these two last Siskins, which apparently were never completed.

The Martlesham trials of the Siskin were flown by Major Oliver Stewart who described it as "gentle, easy-going, calm, good-tempered . . . the outlook was remarkably good and the cockpit arrangements and flying qualities comfortable". The Siskin was, in Major Stewart's words, "extremely easy to fly, and it is probable that it was, at the time it first appeared, the easiest single-seater fighter ever introduced into flying service".

When the R.A.F.8 engine had been revised and built as the Armstrong-Siddeley Jaguar an early example was installed in the Siskin C4541. Thus the aircraft came very close to fulfilling Captain Green's original conception of the S.E.7, yet the Jaguar installation looked less tidy and more makeshift than that of the Dragonfly. With the Jaguar the Siskin had a modified rudder.

Whereas all the other wartime fighters designed for the unsuccessful Dragonfly engine came to nothing, the Siskin was developed into the Armstrong-Whitworth Siskin III and IIIA, both of which were built in large numbers for the Royal Air Force.

**Type:** *Single-seat fighter.* **Power:** *One 320-h.p. A.B.C. Dragonfly nine-cylinder air-cooled radial engine; one 300-h.p. Armstrong Siddeley Jaguar fourteen-cylinder air-cooled radial engine.* **Armament:** *Two fixed, synchronized 0.303-in. Vickers machine-guns.* **Performance:** *Maximum speed 145 m.p.h. at 6,500 ft., 143.5 m.p.h. at 10,000 ft., 139 m.p.h. at 15,000 ft.; climb to 6,500 ft., 4 mins. 30 sec., to 10,000 ft., 7 min. 50 sec., to 15,000 ft., 13 min. 50 sec. Service ceiling 23,800 ft.* **Weights:** *Empty 1,463 lb., loaded 2,181 lb.* **Dimensions:** *Span, upper 27 ft. 6 in.; length, 21 ft. 3 in.; height, 9 ft. 9 in.; wing area 247 sq. ft.*

# SOPWITH TABLOID

The first Sopwith Tabloid appeared in November 1913 as a two-seat sporting biplane. It was a remarkably clean and compact little aircraft and had an unusually good performance on the rather nominal 80 h.p. provided by its Gnome rotary engine. When tested at Farnborough on 29th November 1913, carrying pilot, passenger and fuel for two and a half hours, the little Sopwith had a speed range of 92–36.9 m.p.h. and an initial rate of climb of 1,200 ft. per minute.

Structurally the Tabloid was conventional, being a wire-braced, fabric-covered wooden airframe. The engine was carried in a fore-and-aft mounting, and was cowled in an unusual but quite sensible manner. Pilot and passenger sat side-by-side in dubious comfort, the pilot on the left; their upward outlook was poor, for the cockpit was under the centre section. Lateral control was by wing warping; there was no fin in the tail unit. The first Tabloid weighed no more than 670 lb. empty; with pilot and fuel for 3½ hours it weighed 1,060 lb.

The Tabloid's high performance commended it to the R.F.C. as a possible high-speed scouting aircraft, and a small batch was ordered for the Service. The first was finished early in April 1914; the sixth reached Brooklands on 26th May 1914. Others were to follow. The Tabloid was thus the first single-seat scout to go into production.

These production aircraft were single-seaters and differed from the prototype in some minor respects. The design of the nose was modified slightly, and the tail unit had a fixed fin and plain rudder, similar to those of the Tabloid seaplane that won the Schneider

*The prototype Sopwith Tabloid.*

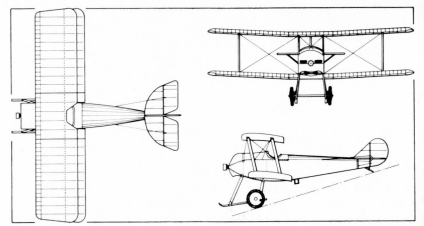

Trophy contest at Monaco in April 1914. The undercarriage skids were longer than those of the prototype and the supporting struts were longer and more raked; at least one Tabloid had its undercarriage strengthened by the introduction of a third strut on each side. Each wheel was borne on its own half-axle in the way that was to become characteristic of virtually all subsequent Sopwith landplanes.

One of the first Tabloids was allotted to No. 7 Squadron R.F.C. in the early summer of 1914, but the unit was broken up to provide additional personnel for Nos. 2, 3, 4, and 5 Squadrons when war broke out. Four Tabloids went to France, in crates, with the Aircraft Park, which arrived at Boulogne on 19th August 1914. Two of these were being flown a week later by Lieutenants Norman Spratt and Gordon Bell, and on the 28th Spratt

succeeded in forcing down an enemy aircraft by circling above it and making feint attacks. His "armament" on that occasion was said to be "a handful of flêchettes", but three days later he took with him a revolver from which he fired thirty shots at an enemy aircraft without success. Nothing daunted, he promptly created a home-made weapon consisting of a hand-grenade on a length of cable: this he intended to entangle in the airscrew of an enemy aircraft. His device was never put to the test, but could be regarded as a forerunner of the Royal Aircraft Factory's Fiery Grapnel.

The Tabloid saw very little operational use. Combats were so few and tentative that lack of effective armament can scarcely have been the main reason for this. It seems more probable that the little Sopwith was somewhat too light to be of practical use under operational

102

*An early production Tabloid for the R.F.C.*

conditions. The type was used briefly by Nos. 3 & 4 Squadrons, R.F.C., but was soon withdrawn.

Some Tabloids were supplied to the R.N.A.S. Commander C. R. Samson's squadron at Antwerp received two, Nos. 167 and 168, late in September. These aircraft, flown by Squadron Commander Spenser Grey and Flight Lieutenant R. L. G. Marix respectively, bombed Cologne and the Düsseldorf airship

*A later Tabloid, No. 1208, at R.N.A.S. Great Yarmouth in 1915. This aircraft had a V-strut undercarriage and ailerons connected by light struts.*

sheds on 7th October. Marix scored the more spectacular success, for his bombs destroyed the new Zeppelin Z.IX.

This was the Tabloid's only feat of arms. Two later Tabloids of Samson's squadron had a Lewis gun on an overwing mounting but apparently had no combats. Four were allotted to No. 1 Squadron, R.N.A.S. in December 1914, but seem to have been little used. Those that went to the Dardanelles aboard the *Ark Royal* in February 1915 were not used operationally.

The two that were taken to Tenedos by Samson's No. 3 Aeroplane Squadron, R.N.A.S., in the following month, did a little flying from the crude aerodrome there but achieved nothing of note.

No real development of the basic design was attempted: the Gordon-Bennett racer was a distinct and separate type. Later Tabloids

had ailerons and a V-type undercarriage, and in the spring of 1915 Tabloid No. 1208 was in this form at the R.N.A.S. station Great Yarmouth.

After the spring of 1915 the Tabloid was not heard of again. A few probably lingered on for training purposes, but the aircraft's apparent potential was never realized. In curious contrast, the single-seat seaplanes derived from the Tabloid served throughout the war.

*Type: Single-seat scout.* **Power:** *80-h.p. Gnome seven-cylinder rotary engine.* **Armament:** *Varied considerably; at best consisted of one 0.303-in. Lewis machine-gun.* **Performance:** *Maximum speed 92 m.p.h. at ground level; initial rate of climb 1,200 ft./min.; endurance $3\frac{1}{2}$ hours.* **Weights:** *Empty 730 lb., loaded 1,120 lb.* **Dimensions:** *Span, 25 ft. 6 in.; length, 20 ft. 4 in.; height, 8 ft. 5 in.; wing area, 241.3 sq. ft.*

# SOPWITH GORDON BENNETT RACERS

The fact that aircraft design had advanced so far by the time war broke out in 1914 can be attributed, in part at least, to the stimulus provided by the various major prize contests that were held from 1909 onwards. In that year James Gordon Bennett, publisher of the *New York Herald*, offered a trophy and a purse of £1,000 for the highest speed attained by an aircraft over a defined course; the contest was to be held annually and was international.

No British entry was made for the 1913 contest, which was won at Rheims on 29th September by the beautiful Deperdussin monoplane flown by Prévost at an average speed of 124.5 m.p.h. In 1914 the Sopwith company built a clean little biplane for the Gordon Bennett race to be held that year. This was a highly optimistic venture: not only did the Sopwith compare unfavourably with

the exceptionally clean Deperdussin monoplane of 1913, but its power unit was only an 80-h.p. Gnome.

This engine was closely and cleanly cowled, and the slim fuselage had side fairings that extended as far aft as the tailplane. The symmetrical fin and rudder looked perilously small. The wings appeared to be standard Tabloid surfaces but had no stagger; the interplane and centre-section struts were of streamline-section steel tubing. A simple V-type undercarriage was fitted.

The outbreak of war prevented the Gordon Bennett contest from taking place. The Sopwith entrant was a potential high-speed scout and was taken over by the R.N.A.S. with the serial number 1215. It was at Hendon in November 1914 but seems to have found no operational use.

No. 1214 with fixed
Lewis gun and armoured
airscrew with bullet de-
flectors.

Lt. Spenser Grey with
No. 1215 at Hendon.

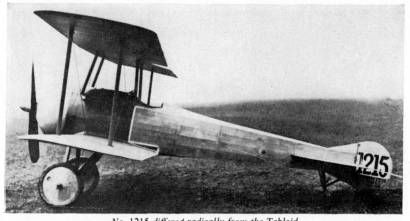

*No. 1215 differed radically from the Tabloid.*

Linked with this special Gordon Bennett racing aircraft was another Sopwith single-seater which, on being taken over by the R.N.A.S., was given the serial number 1214. It, too, has been listed as a "Sopwith Gordon Bennett" and may have been the Sopwith company's second string for the contest, but it was very different from 1215.

No. 1214 was virtually indistinguishable from a Tabloid, but it was powered by a 100-h.p. Gnome Monosoupape in a bullnose cowling similar to that of the Tabloid but with five intake slots in its upper half. The V-struts of its undercarriage were narrow and resembled those of 1215 more than those of the earlier landplane conversion of the original Schneider-winning Tabloid. The wings of No. 1214, like those of No. 1215, appeared to be standard Tabloid components, and the struts were of steel tubing.

The R.N.A.S. sent No. 1214 to France, where it was used at the R.N.A.S. station, Dunkerque, and was still in service there in June 1915. By that time it was armed with a fixed Lewis gun on the starboard side and its airscrew was fitted with the steel deflectors then in use on some contemporary Morane-Saulnier fighting aircraft. It had also acquired large wing-tip skids.

**Type:** *Single-seat scout.* **Power:** *No. 1214 had a 100-h.p. Gnome Monosoupape nine-cylinder rotary engine, No. 1215 an 80-h.p. Gnome seven-cylinder rotary.* **Armament:** *No. 1214 had a single, fixed 0.303-in. Lewis machine-gun.* **Performance:** *No. 1215 was reported to have a speed of 105 m.p.h.* **Weights:** *No details available.* **Dimensions:** *Span, probably about 25 ft. 6 in.; wing area about 241 sq. ft.*

# SOPWITH GUN BUSES

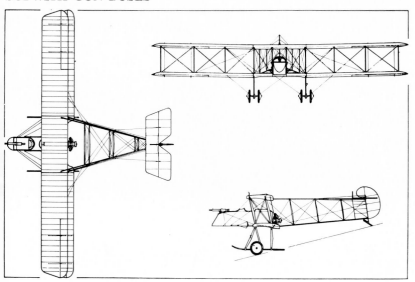

The Sopwith Gun Buses had their origins in a series of single-engine pusher seaplanes that apparently began with the Hydro Biplane Type S, a large aircraft of 80 ft. span and a designed all-up weight of 5,230 lb., armed with a quick-firing gun. It may have been the Sopwith seaplane Gun Bus, powered by a 120-h.p. Austro-Daimler, that had the official serial number 93.

Early in 1914 the Sopwith company delivered to the Greek government a pusher seaplane powered by a 100-h.p. Anzani radial engine. This was used for training purposes at Eleusis, and in March the Greek government ordered six more aircraft of the same type, but specified the provision of a machine-gun mounted on the nose of the nacelle. To meet this requirement the Sopwith S.P.Gn was designed in April 1914. This aircraft embodied the mainplanes, tailplane, elevators and floats of the Anzani pusher, but the nacelle was revised to accommodate in the forward cockpit a gunner,

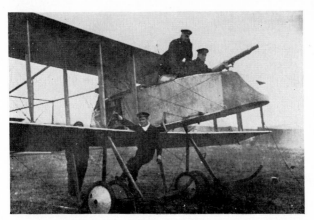

for whom a Lewis machine-gun was provided; the engine was to be a 100-h.p. Gnome Monosoupape. Span was 50 ft., the empty weight 1,600 lb., loaded weight 2,360 lb.

Construction of the six Greek gun-carriers went ahead during the summer of 1914, and the fourth was reported to have been test-flown at Woolston on 23rd June. When war broke out in August 1914 the aircraft were promptly commandeered by the British Admiralty. They were probably the Sopwith aircraft that were given the serial numbers 896–901; these serials fall among a group of assorted aircraft, mostly privately owned, that were impressed on the outbreak of war for use by the R.N.A.S. Some at least of these Sopwiths may have been taken over as seaplanes, for in *The Story of a North Sea Air Station*, C. F. Snowden Gamble records that in September 1914 there were only eight aircraft on the strength of Great Yarmouth Air Station, of which four were the Sopwith seaplanes Nos. 880, 897, 898 and 899, all with 100 b.h.p. Gnome engines. The last three machines were classified as "Gun Machines" and "Bomb Droppers"; earlier that month they had been at R.N.A.S. Calshot.

A landplane version existed, and was the first aircraft to be known as the Sopwith Gun Bus. It was almost identical with the S.P.Gn. but its tail differed from that depicted in the design drawings of the seaplane; the tailplane had a straight leading edge, a fin was fitted under the tailplane, and the rudder was horn balanced. The undercarriage was a simple structure: two skids were attached to the outboard ends of the lower centre section by three struts; each skid was braced by cables to the spars of the lower wings and had a pair of wheels lashed to it by rubber shock-cords. At

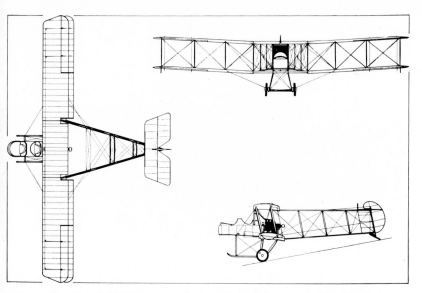

least one Gun Bus of this kind was used at Hendon, armed with a single Lewis gun on a pivoting mounting.

Specifically for the R.N.A.S. a more powerful version of the Sopwith Gun Bus was built. Much of the structure was identical with that of the Monosoupape aircraft, but the roots of the wing panels had a small cut-out to clear the tail-booms, the chord of the lower centre section was reduced, the elevators were strengthened, and the balance area of the rudder was reduced. The major differences in the new type lay in the nacelle and under-carriage, and were necessitated by the heavier and more powerful 150-h.p. Sunbeam engine that replaced the Monosoupape of the earlier version. The nacelle was a completely new structure, in which the pilot's cockpit was wholly ahead of the wings; it was raised slightly above the lower centre section, whereas that of the S.P.Gn. and its landplane derivative had been attached directly to the centre section. The revised undercarriage was of narrower track, having only two wheels and a cross axle.

Six Sunbeam-powered Gun Buses, numbered 801–806, were built by the Sopwith company

109

*Early example of the second type of Sopwith Gun Bus, which had a 150-h.p. Sunbeam engine also, photographed at Hendon.*

with the official designation Admiralty Type 806. Of these, No. 805 is known to have been used for a time by the R.N.A.S. at Hendon. A Sopwith Gun Bus of some kind was, on 6th February 1915, on the strength of the R.N.A.S. squadron at Dunkerque under Commander C. R. Samson. On that date he reported that his Sopwith required "a lot of work on it to make it safe to fly".

A batch of thirty Sunbeam Gun Buses were ordered from Robey & Co., Ltd., of Lincoln. These aircraft were allotted the serial numbers 3833–3862 and differed from the original Sopwith 806 design. The pilot was moved forward to the front cockpit, the nose of the nacelle being extended to accommodate the flight controls; a deep forward decking made the modified nacelle an ugly thing. A transparent panel was let into the floor of the pilot's cockpit and four substantial bomb-carriers were

*Robey-built Sopwith Gun Bus No. 3833, an example of the later form of the Sunbeam powered aircraft in which the pilot occupied the front cockpit and bomb racks were fitted under the lower wings.*

standard fittings under the lower wings: it is possible that the span of the tailplane was increased.

These modifications suggest that the revised Gun Bus was intended for bombing or, possibly, anti-submarine duties rather than fighting. The service history of the type remains obscure, however; it is known that No. 3849 was at Eastchurch at one time and that No. 3838 was still in use during the winter of 1915–16. The fact that only seventeen of the Robey-built aircraft were delivered fully assembled, the remainder as spares, suggests that it was realised at an early stage that the big pusher was not likely to be successful.

**Type:** *Two-seat fighter.* **Power:** *First version, one 100-h.p. Gnome Monosoupape nine-cylinder rotary engine; second version, one 150-h.p. Sunbeam eight-cylinder water-cooled engine.* **Armament:** *One 0.303-in. Lewis machine-gun.* **Performance:** *(Sunbeam) Maximum speed 80 m.p.h.* **Weights:** *No details available.* **Dimensions:** *Span, 50 ft.; length, (Gnome) 32 ft. 9 in., (Sunbeam) 32 ft. 6 in.; height, (Sunbeam) 11 ft. 4 in.; wing area, (Gnome) 480 sq. ft., (Sunbeam) 474 sq. ft.*

# SOPWITH TWO-SEATER SCOUT ("SPINNING JENNY")

*Sopwith two-seater No. 1053 of R.N.A.S. Great Yarmouth, 1915.*

In May 1914 the Sopwith company designed a two-seat tractor biplane, powered by a 100-h.p. Gnome Monosoupape and designated Sopwith D3. Design drawings of this aircraft with a wheel undercarriage were initialled by Herbert Smith on 5th May; drawings of a floatplane version bear the date 19th May. The two-bay wings spanned 36 ft. 6 in., had inversely tapered ailerons and were slightly staggered; the overall length was 27 ft. 6 in. on wheels, 30 ft. 9½ in. on floats.

The aircraft was built, differing from the original design only in having head fairings between the cockpits and behind the pilot's cockpit. It was one of the Sopwith company's two entries in the 1914 Circuit of Britain seaplane competition, but it first appeared with the wheel undercarriage at Brooklands on Wednesday 15th July 1914. It was flown at Brooklands by Victor Mahl, who was to be its pilot in the seaplane contest. The outbreak of war led inevitably to the cancellation of the competition, and it is doubtful whether the Sopwith D3 ever had its floats fitted. One report suggests that an enlarged fin and rudder had been fitted by the beginning of August.

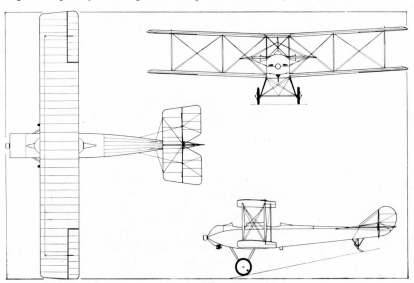

*Spinning Jenny of R.N.A.S. Hendon with taller undercarriage and bomb rack under fuselage.*

Drawings of a modified landplane, still designated D3, have survived. This development had increased gap, a simple V-strut undercarriage, a slightly lengthened fuselage, and enlarged vertical tail surfaces. It is unlikely that this second Sopwith D3 was built, but it provided the design link between the 1914 Circuit of Britain aircraft and the Sopwith 807 seaplane (which will be described in the volume dealing with seaplanes and flying boats of the war period).

The Sopwith 807 appeared in two slightly different versions, and in March 1915 there appeared a Sopwith landplane that was a hybrid development of the 807 and the revised D3 design. Its forward fuselage and cockpit area appeared to be identical with those of the 807 seaplane; the main planes were of equal span and, like those of the 807, had no stagger although they did not fold. Whereas all its antecedents had had the 100-h.p. Gnome Monosoupape the new aircraft was powered by the 80-h.p. Gnome.

Two dozen examples of this aircraft were supplied to the R.N.A.S. with the serial numbers 1051–1074, the last being received at R.N.A.S. Chingford on 28th June 1915. The type was officially known as the Sopwith two-

seater scout, but it was a most unwarlike aeroplane and enjoyed no operational success of any kind.

It was used in small numbers from the R.N.A.S. stations at Hendon, Chingford, Great Yarmouth and Killingholme. Those flown from Hendon had a rack for small bombs between the rear legs of the undercarriage V-struts. The undercarriages of aircraft fitted with these bomb racks were made taller than that of the basic design. The Sopwith two-seaters of Great Yarmouth made coastal patrols, armed in thoroughly makeshift manner. The following quotation from *The Story of a North Sea Air Station* speaks for itself:

"The machines were armed with a Service rifle fitted with Hale grenades, and a shotgun firing chain shot, and a Véry light with two rounds of ammunition; this latter was considered the best weapon of offence. So loaded, with an observer sitting in a seat where he could see nothing and use none of his equipment, these Sopwiths might, if properly handled, attain 3,000 ft. Owing to the shape of the engine cowl the Gnome engine got very hot, so forced landings occurred on 50 per cent of the trips."

The Sopwith's flying qualities left a good deal to be desired, for it would spin at the slightest provocation and quickly became known as the Spinning Jenny in the R.N.A.S. In his first spin on the type Flt.-Lt. J. C. Brooke of R.N.A.S. Killingholme managed to regain control, and on the following day he did two deliberate spins, flying No. 1055, and recovered from both after losing about 1,000 ft. He was thus possibly the first man to perform and recover from an intentional spin.

It may have been these dangerous characteristics that led to the fitting of an enlarged fin and tailplane to the aircraft. Some of the Sopwiths at Hendon had the new surfaces by mid-April 1915.

It seems unlikely that the Spinning Jenny remained in active use much beyond 1915. Nevertheless, rigging diagrams and instructions for the aircraft were included in an official R.N.A.S. handbook, *Truing-up of Aeroplanes*, which was dated as late as 1st September 1916. Some were used for training purposes at Chingford but the type was clearly unsuitable for such duties.

**Type:** *Two-seat Home Defence fighter.* **Power:** *One 80-h.p. Gnome seven-cylinder rotary engine.* **Armament:** *Various combinations of* rifles, shot-guns, Véry pistols, or Mauser rifles firing incendiary ammunition. A few light bombs could be carried under the fuselage. **Performance:** *Maximum speed 69 m.p.h. at* ground level; climb to 3,000 ft., 20 min.; ceiling 3,000 ft.; endurance 2½ hours. **Weights:** *No details available.* **Dimensions:** *Span, 36 ft.*

## SOPWITH 1½ STRUTTER

To the Sopwith 1½ Strutter belongs the distinction of being the first true two-seat fighter of tractor layout to see service. It was also the first Sopwith type to carry the unmistakable stamp of the design team that included R. J. Ashfield and Herbert Smith, and was in its day a remarkably advanced aircraft.

The 1½ Strutter was designed and built for the Admiralty; the prototype, No. 3686, was passed by the Sopwith experimental depart-

ment on 12th December 1915. It was a handsome single-bay biplane, powered by a 110-h.p. Clerget 9Z rotary engine that ran on an overhung mounting. The airframe was conventionally built of wood, with wire cross bracing and fabric covering. The halves of the upper wing met at the centre line (there was no upper centre section) and were supported by the characteristic arrangement of struts from which the aircraft derived its nickname. The

*Unarmed and wearing no serial number, this 1½ Strutter is thought to be the prototype.*

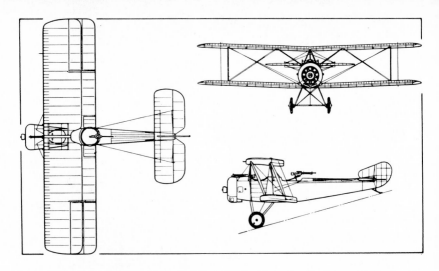

lower wings were attached to stub wings that incorporated airbrakes, pivoted surfaces that moved upwards to present a flat surface to the airstream. An innovation of some significance was the adjustable tailplane; its incidence could be varied in flight by a handwheel in the pilot's cockpit.

This prototype was unarmed but fortunately the 1½ Strutter was completed at the time when successful British gun-synchronizing mechanisms and the ingenious and efficient Scarff No. 2 Ring Mounting became available. The Vickers-Challenger synchronizing gear was functioning in December 1915 and was quickly put into production for the R.F.C.; the Scarff-Dibovski gear was tested early in

1916 and was ordered in quantity for the R.N.A.S. The Scarff ring mounting for the observer's gun also went into production for the R.N.A.S. early in 1916.

The first production contract for the 1½ Strutter was placed by the Admiralty, and deliveries began in February 1916. The earliest aircraft had no fixed gun for the pilot, doubtless owing to the prevailing shortage of Vickers guns that did not begin to be eased until that February; and alternative mountings for the Lewis gun were fitted until Scarff rings became available. A few aircraft, such as A377, had an adjustable cranked pillar mounting for the observer's gun; others had the cumbersome Nieuport mounting. The

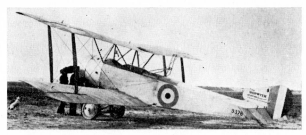

*The first production aircraft, No. 9376, with a Nieuport gun mounting on the observer's cockpit; no Vickers gun was fitted when this photograph was taken. This 1½ Strutter was used by No. 5 Wing, R.N.A.S., when it was fully armed with Vickers gun and a Scarff No. 2 mounting for the observer's Lewis gun. It made a forced landing in Holland on 22nd April* 1917 *and was thereafter used by the Dutch* Luchtvaart Afdeling *as LA-42.*

official Admiralty designation for the aircraft was Sopwith Type 9400.

A single-seat bomber version of the 1½ Strutter was built at the same time as the two-seater; its Admiralty designation was Sopwith Type 9700. Some of these single-seat bombers were converted into two-seat fighters. The single-seat 1½ Strutter bomber will be described in the companion volume on bomber aircraft of the first world war.

By the end of April 1916, No. 5 Wing, R.N.A.S., had one complete Flight of the new

Sopwith two-seaters and deliveries from the Sopwith-built batches 9376–9425 and 9651–9750 grew steadily in volume. The War Office had ordered the type for the R.F.C. but had had to place its contracts with other manufacturers. The first six 1½ Strutters for the R.F.C. (5719–5721 and 7998–8000) were at Farnborough in the last week of April, but were apparently aircraft transferred from R.N.A.S. contracts. The first production aircraft built by Ruston Proctor & Co. (7762) did not reach Farnborough until 20th

*No.* 7942 *was a singleton transfer from the R.N.A.S. to the R.F.C. It was at Farnborough on* 14th June 1916, *and was subsequently used by R.F.C. Squadrons Nos.* 52 *and* 70. *When photographed it had a Nieuport ring mounting on the rear cockpit and the pilot's gun apparently mounted on the starboard upper longeron.*

*A standard production 1½ Strutter, N5624, built by Westland Aircraft, with Scarff No. 2 ring mounting on the rear cockpit.*

July 1916; the first Vickers-built machine (A1054) was reported to be there ten days later.

The spring of 1916 was an anxious time for the R.F.C. An assessment of its needs to meet the demands of the great Somme offensive that was planned for 29th June 1916 (subsequently postponed to 1st July) showed it to be critically short of aircraft. So urgent was the need for fighting aircraft that No. 70 Squadron, the first to be equipped with 1½ Strutters, went to France Flight by Flight as each was brought up to strength: 'A' Flight on 24th May, 'B' on 29th June, 'C' on 30th July. Its aircraft had been transferred from R.N.A.S. contracts, the first of the seventy-seven 1½ Strutters handed over by the Admiralty during the summer of 1916 in response to the urgent appeal for assistance for the R.F.C. made by Major-General Trenchard in May 1916. The ex-R.N.A.S. aircraft were re-numbered (e.g. A377–A386, A878–A897, A1902–A1931, A2983–A2991). Things did not apparently move with all the speed that the circumstances demanded, however. It is known that A380–A385 were allocated to 'B' Flight of No. 70 Squadron, which did not cross the Channel until 29th June—yet at least the first five of these six 1½ Strutters were at Farnborough as early as 6th June.

For several weeks the Sopwiths of No. 70 Squadron gave a good account of themselves, their long range enabling them to penetrate far into enemy territory. But by the time No. 45 Squadron arrived in France on 15th October

*Some 1½ Strutters were built as single-seaters, but not as single-seat bombers. One such was the first Morgan-built 1½ Strutter, A5950.*

1916 new German single-seaters, heavily armed, had been introduced. From the autumn of 1916 onwards the 1½ Strutters' effectiveness declined, and by the time No. 43 Squadron reached France on 17th January, 1917, the Sopwiths were outclassed and their losses grew.

Perhaps the 1½ Strutter might have retained combat effectiveness longer if it had been more manoeuvrable. The C.F.S. report on the type stated "Machine is rather heavy and slow on controls"; Captain Norman Macmillan wrote "We had to exert all our strength and skill to make them dive, for they were very stable and resisted any sudden change in flight attitude". It could not hope to match the agility of the new Albatros and Halberstadt single-seaters.

The type was not finally superseded by the Camel until early October 1917, and the gallant two-seaters did much good work, obsolete though they were, through the Battles of Arras, Messines and Ypres.

Later production 1½ Strutters had the 130 h.p. Clerget engine. The Ross interrupter gear and Sopwith-Kauper synchronizing gear were fitted to the pilot's armament in some aircraft.

In September 1916 a variant of the 1½

*Home Defence single-seat fighter conversion of the 1½ Strutter, known as the Sopwith Comic. B762 was used at Sutton's Farm, almost certainly by No. 78 Squadron, and was normally armed with twin Lewis guns on a double Foster mounting on the upper wing.*

Strutter powered by the 150-h.p. Smith Static engine was designed. The Admiralty had become interested in this unusual ten-cylinder radial engine early in 1915 and conducted exhaustive tests of it; possibly the modified 1½ Strutter was intended to be a test-bed for the Smith, but it is not known whether the installation was made. The loaded weight of the aircraft with fuel for four hours was expected to be 1,960 lb.

The R.F.C. used 1½ Strutters for Home Defence purposes in 1917; the type was flown by squadrons Nos. 37, 44 and 78. Fifty-six 1½ Strutter two-seaters and three single-seaters were allocated to Home Defence units; the latter may have been some of those aircraft on R.F.C. contracts that were built without an observer's cockpit (e.g. A5950) and externally resembled the bomber form of the 1½ Strutter. Several of the two-seaters were converted into single-seaters of an entirely different kind in which the pilot occupied what would ordinarily have been the rear cockpit, the front cockpit being faired over. This was a "home-made" development of the 1½ Strutter evolved by Captain F. W. Honnett of No. 78 Squadron, where it was known as the Sopwith Comic. The armament of these Home Defence conversions varied considerably. At least one, A6906, had originally had a single Vickers gun in the standard position above the nose; later, in common with other Sopwith Comics of No. 78 Squadron, this aircraft had a single Lewis gun mounted centrally above the upper wing and firing forward over the airscrew. When B762 was tested at Martlesham Heath it had a pair of Lewis guns on a special mounting in front of the cockpit, firing upward.

R.N.A.S. 1½ Strutters were used as fighters and as bombers, and in the latter capacity had some considerable success. Only the R.N.A.S. used the 1½ Strutter outside the French theatre of war: in the Aegean area 'A', 'B', 'C' and 'D' squadrons all had a few Sopwiths on their strength, and in March 1917 'E' and 'F' Squadrons had some 1½ Strutters when they were formed. These aircraft did more bombing than fighting, however.

The R.N.A.S. also used 1½ Strutters as shipboard aircraft, but their function was reconnaissance and their history, embodying many experiments with undercarriages and flotation gear, is appropriate to another volume.

France, Belgium and Russia used the 1½ Strutter, and both versions of the design were produced on a very large scale in France. Some of the French-built aircraft had the 110-h.p. Le Rhône 9J, 135-h.p. Le Rhône 9Jby,

*Le Rhône-powered 1½ Strutter with ski undercarriage in service in Russia.*

120

135-h.p. Clerget 9Ba, 135-h.p. Clerget 9Bb or 145-h.p. Clerget 9Bc as alternative engines. The two-seat 1½ Strutter was manufactured in Russia by the Dux company of Moscow and by V. A. Lebedev of Novaya Derevna, St. Petersburg. The first Lebedev contract, dated 1st July 1917, was for 50 Sopwiths; it was followed by a later order for 140 further aircraft. The Russian-built 1½ Strutters had modified undercarriages of Russian design. Owing to a chronic lack of engines, few Russian-built 1½ Strutters entered service.

These Allied countries used the Sopwith primarily as a reconnaissance or bomber aircraft, but it is of interest to record that the leading Belgian fighter pilot, Baron Coppens de Houthulst, flew the Mann Egerton 1½ Strutter N5240 while he was with the Belgian 4th Squadron. Five of the 1½ Strutters that came down in Dutch territory (including the first production aircraft, No. 9376) were flown by the Dutch *Luchtvaart Afdeling* from 1917 onwards. A few specimens were flown by Roumania and Japan.

Possibly the last 1½ Strutters in operational use were those flown for a short time between May and July 1918 by the U.S. 88th, 90th and 99th Aero Squadrons. The American Expeditionary Force had bought 514 1½ Strutters from France in the spring of 1918, but used most of them as trainers at Issoudun.

At home the 1½ Strutter was flown at various experimental stations, including Biggin Hill, where two of the Sopwiths pioneered the use of air-to-air radio telephony. The type ended its service with training units, and a few were used by senior officers as personal aircraft. Notable among these was B8912, which was used by Lieutenant-Colonel R. R. Smith-Barry, the creator and Commanding Officer of the School of Special Flying, Gosport.

**Type:** *Two-seat fighter reconnaissance.* **Power:** *One 110-h.p. Clerget 9Z, 130-h.p. Clerget 9B, 135-h.p. Clerget 9Ba, 135-h.p. Clerget 9Bb, 145-h.p. Clerget 9Bc, 110-h.p. Le Rhône 9J, 135-h.p. Le Rhône 9Jby: all were nine-cylinder rotary engines.* **Armament:** *One fixed, synchronized 0.303-in. Vickers machine-gun; one 0.303-in. Lewis gun. Armament of Home Defence 1½ Strutters varied.* **Performance** (*with 130-h.p. Clerget*): *Maximum speed 100 m.p.h. at 6,500 ft., 97.5 m.p.h. at 10,000 ft.; climb to 6,500 ft., 9 min. 10 sec.; to 10,000 ft., 17 min. 50 sec.; service ceiling 15,500 ft.; endurance 3¾ hours.* **Weights** (*130-h.p. Clerget*): *Empty 1,305 lb., loaded 2,150 lb.* **Dimensions:** *Span, 33 ft. 6 in., length 25 ft. 3 in., height, 10 ft. 3 in.; wing area 346 sq. ft.*

# SOPWITH PUP

The Sopwith Pup was a masterpiece. No other aircraft of the war period combined so much aesthetic appeal and such delightful handling qualities; few could equal its performance on the 80-h.p. Le Rhône engine. Its name was, of course, unofficial; and the identity of the man who first called it the Pup seems not to have been recorded.

Structurally there was nothing unconventional about the Pup. The fuselage had ash longerons and spruce spacers, and was a conventional wire-braced box girder with fabric covering over most of its length. The wings had spruce spars and ribs, and the small ailerons were hinged to the rear spars. Steel tubing of varying sizes was used to make the fin, rudder and elevators; the wooden tailplane

had a steel-tube rear spar. A simple V-type undercarriage incorporating the Sopwith divided axle was fitted.

In appearance the Pup bore an obvious resemblance to the 1½ Strutter, but it also incorporated some of the characteristics of the little single-seat biplane that had been built in 1915 as a personal aircraft for Harry Hawker. In the air the Pup could easily be recognised by the distinctive plan-form of its wing tips and tailplane.

The prototype Pup, No. 3691, was flying in the spring of 1916. In May it went to 'A' Squadron, R.N.A.S., at Furnes for Service evaluation, and instantly delighted the Naval pilots with its speed, manoeuvrability and good performance. Five further prototypes, num-

*Pup No. 9497 at the Isle of Grain, 7th December 1916. This aircraft had an 80-h.p. Clerget engine and had been flown at the Dalmuir works of William Beardmore & Co., Ltd., as early as 5th October 1916. It was delivered to the Isle of Grain on 1st November, and was extensively used in early deck-landing experiments there.*

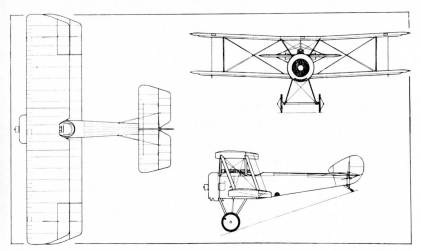

bered 9496, 9497 and 9898–9900, were built; all had the 80-h.p. Clerget engine.

Both the Admiralty and the War Office placed substantial orders for the Pup, the former with the Sopwith and Beardmore companies, the latter with the Standard Motor Co. and Whitehead Aircraft, Ltd. Production aircraft did not begin to appear until September, the first specimens being supplied to the R.N.A.S. The first eleven Beardmore-built Pups had the 80-h.p. Clerget engine, but the 80-h.p. Le Rhône was fitted to subsequent aircraft and was the standard power unit for the type. In addition to the aircraft ordered from Admiralty contractors, the R.N.A.S. received a few of the Pups ordered under R.F.C. contracts.

It seems that No. 1 Wing R.N.A.S. received the first production Pups. Late in October 1916 this unit provided six to equip one Flight of No. 8 Squadron R.N.A.S., and by 16th November the other two Flights had exchanged their Nieuports and 1½ Strutters for Pups. In action the Pup soon showed its mettle and Naval Eight built up an impressive score of combat successes.

The first R.F.C. unit to have the Pup was No. 54 Squadron, which arrived in France on 24th December 1916. Squadrons Nos. 46 and 66 also flew the type, as did Naval Squadrons Nos. 3, 4 and 9. So well did the Pups of No. 3 Naval Squadron acquit themselves during the Battles of Arras in the spring of 1917 that the official historian wrote: ". . . the losses they

*Standard Whitehead-built Pup for the R.F.C. This aircraft was reported to be at Farnborough on 17th February 1917.*

inflicted were such as to cause the enemy pilots to avoid them in the air whenever they could."

By the late summer of 1917 the Pup was obsolescent as a front-line fighter. Various attempts were made in Squadrons Nos. 54 and 66 to augment the armament by mounting a Lewis gun above the centre section, but these were mostly unsuccessful. Nevertheless, although the opposing fighters of autumn 1917 had more power and better armament, the Pup was useful to the end of its operational life, for its height-holding capabilities were better than those of the later D.H.5. It retained its remarkable manoeuvrability even at 15,000 ft.

Enemy bombing attacks on London led first to the brief withdrawal to Calais of No. 66 Squadron, and later to the transfer of No. 46 Squadron from France to Sutton's Farm on 10th July 1917. Two additional Pup squadrons were formed for Home Defence duties, No. 61 on 2nd August and No. 112 on 30th July.

To give the Pup the necessary performance to combat the Gotha bombers that had begun to attack England in daylight, the 100-h.p. Gnome Monosoupape was fitted to some of the Home Defence aircraft. This engine had a cowling of longer chord, open at the bottom

*Pup B1755 with 100-h.p. Gnome Monosoupape engine.*

and provided with four slots in its upper starboard quadrant. The Monosoupape-powered Pup had an improved rate of climb and a slightly higher ceiling than the Le Rhône version; some had the Constantinesco gun-synchronizing gear.

At least one Monosoupape-powered Pup, A653, had a sketchier engine cowling than was standard, and its Vickers gun was mounted above the port upper longeron. Some attempts were made to fit a Lewis gun to Home Defence Pups, but met with no more success than earlier efforts of the squadrons in France.

The Pups of the first Sopwith-built R.N.A.S.

*N5186 (80-h.p. Le Rhône) fitted with eight Le Prieur rockets, Eastchurch, 25th October 1916.*

*One of the few two-gun Pups was this Beardmore-built aircraft of 'C' Squadron, R.N.A.S., Imbros, which combined the Lewis mounting of a Sopwith 9901 with the Vickers installation of a standard Pup.*

batch (N5180–N5199) had the same centre section as the R.F.C.'s aircraft. Later R.N.A.S. Pups had a modified centre section with a central aperture between the spars to permit the installation of an upward-firing Lewis gun for anti-airship purposes. This R.N.A.S. ver-

sion of the Pup was designated Sopwith 9901 by the Admiralty. Beardmore-built Pups could have three different arrangements of armament: the Lewis gun alone; Lewis gun plus eight Le Prieur rockets; or the rockets alone. In the last-mentioned form the centre section was faired over.

At least one Sopwith 9901 had what must have been the only really successful installation of Vickers and Lewis guns and is illustrated here. It was used by "C" Squadron of the R.N.A.S. operating from Imbros in the Aegean theatre of war.

Thanks to the initiative and advocacy of Flight Commander F. J. Rutland the Pup came into use as a shipboard fighter early in 1917 and was used on the aircraft carriers *Manxman*, *Furious* and *Campania*. In June 1917 Rutland made a successful take-off from a 20 ft. platform on the light cruiser *Yarmouth*; on 17th August 1917 it was decided to

*No. 9497 in one of its later guises with fixed skid undercarriage at the Isle of Grain, 8th March 1918. Production shipboard Pups with this undercarriage were designated Sopwith 9901a.*

*Another Pup used in deck-landing experiments was N6190, seen here with forward extensions on its skids and an arrester hook under the fuselage. This photograph was taken on 20th September 1918 in the course of experiments with arrester cables on the dummy deck at Grain.*

fit one ship in each light-cruiser squadron with a flying-off deck. As if to emphasize the rightness of this decision, Flight Sub-Lieutenant B. A. Smart, flying *Yarmouth's* Pup, shot down the Zeppelin L.23 on 21st August 1917.

Aircraft flown off these tiny shipboard platforms were fitted with flotation gear, for they had no choice but to ditch at the end of their flight. The first Beardmore Pup, 9901, was used in early experiments with the Mark I Emergency Flotation Bags. In May 1917, fitted with the air bags and a jettisonable undercarriage, it was successfully ditched off the Isle of Grain.

Experiments with aircraft-launching catapults were conducted in 1917 at Hendon, whence two Beardmore Pups (Nos. 9948 and 9949) were sent direct from the Dalmuir factory in May 1917, specifically for these trials. It is believed that one was successfully launched from a catapult designed by R. F. Carey. Development of the technique was not pressed, however, largely because the Pup had itself demonstrated that shipboard aircraft could be flown from small platforms.

Thought had already been given to the problems of landing on a carrier vessel. As early as March 1917 the Pups 9912 and 9497 had been used in deck-landing tests, using a

*Pup fitted with tandem grooved wheels under each lower wing. These wheels were intended to run along parallel wire cables mounted horizontally above a ship's fo'c's'le, enabling the aircraft to take off without the need for a full flight deck.*

dummy deck on the aerodrome at the Isle of Grain. Landing on a ship under way was more hazardous. The first successful landings of this

kind were made on 2nd and 7th August 1917 by Squadron Commander E. H. Dunning, who landed his Pup on the forward deck of H.M.S. *Furious*. This feat testified both to Dunning's skill and the controllability of the aircraft, for the deck lay forward of the central funnel and superstructure. Dunning was drowned in N6452 in attempting a further landing on 7th August.

Although no further landings on ships at sea were made in 1917, experiments with deck-landing equipment continued at the Isle of Grain under the supervision of Squadron Commander Harry Busteed. Arrester cables and hooks were tested and, almost oddly, the experiments produced the Sopwith 9901a, a ship's Pup with plain wooden skids instead of wheels. Several types of skids, sprung and rigid, were tested, in combination with an astonishing variety of devices to engage arrester cables; as an alternative, a Pup with steel-shod skids was tested on a magnetic deck, but this idea apparently came to naught. Ultimately rigid skids with small horns that engaged under close-set fore-and-aft cables were more or less standardized. Yet in October 1918 the Pup flown by Lt. Arnold in deck-landing trials on H.M.S. *Argus* had a wheel undercarriage; nine V-clips were fixed under the spreader bar, and a curved guard protected the airscrew. At that time the Isle of Grain was experimenting with the Armstrong-Whitworth arrester gear, which consisted of athwartships cables engaged by an arrester hook; the trials included Pups with skid and wheel undercarriages. At Grain N6190, fitted with various forms of skid undercarriages, was frequently used in the experiments; and when tests were made aboard H.M.S. *Furious* in April 1918 the Pups 9949 and C214, with skid undercarriages, were used and sustained varying amounts of damage.

In other deck-flying experiments aimed at facilitating take-off from ships under way, deep wooden troughs for the Pup's wheels were tried out; these were fitted to some carriers. One aircraft was fitted with a tandem pair of small, deeply-grooved wheels under each lower wing. These wheels were intended to run on parallel wire jack-stays raised above a ship's deck; take-off over the fo'c's'le was envisaged. Presumably it was hoped by this means to dispense with the conventional undercarriage altogether, but the idea was clearly impracticable.

The shipboard Pups were largely replaced

by 2F.1 Camels, but at the end of October 1918 ten Sopwith 9901a's and thirteen 9901s were still operational. Elsewhere the Pup had given excellent and popular service as a training aircraft, sometimes with the 80-h.p. Gnome or Clerget engine replacing the Le Rhône. Many became the personal aircraft of senior officers; all were loved by those who flew them.

Production had continued long after the Pup's withdrawal from squadrons in France, and the type was still being manufactured in the autumn of 1918. In all, over 1,800 were built. A late official task for the Pup was its use as a test vehicle, in company with a Salamander, for experimental camouflage paint schemes. The tests were conducted in the summer of 1918, the aircraft being painted with irregular patches of dark purple earth, green, light earth, light green-grey and black.

Declared obsolete in December 1918, the Pup disappeared quickly. Some went to Australia as part of the Imperial Gift; a few acquired civil identities. One or two lingered on in official service; B7565 was still in use at Farnborough in September 1919, testing the gravity ground ndicator, presumably a kind of automatic landing aid allied to the Pale-thorpe and Noakes devices.

At the Isle of Grain Wing Commander Harry Bustced continued to fly his Pup B2217 at least until February 1920, and other Pups remained in use there that year in remarkable experiments that aimed at extending the usefulness of aircraft at sea. To facilitate liaison with ships not equipped as aircraft carriers, Pups and Camels were fitted with a hook above the centre section; this was intended to engage with a loop running along a cable stretched between two booms carried outboard of the ship. Wing loadings and stalling speeds of that period allowed the relative speed between ship and aircraft to be small, but clearly wind and weather conditions would have imposed severe restrictions on the use of the device. Successful "landings" were made on a rig at the Isle of Grain by Wing Commander E. L. Gerrard in a Pup in mid-1920; the first may have been the success recorded on 15th June of that year, but as early as 2nd March, Harry Busteed had flown a Pup on what he recorded

*Pup with overwing hook for experiments in landing on cables, Isle of Grain, 1920.*

as "Practice at landing on single wire (overhead)". The aircraft was his own B2217.

A single example of the Pup was used by the Dutch Luchtvaart Afdeling. This aircraft, A6164, landed in Holland on 1st March 1917 and was interned. In Dutch service its number was LA 41. A few Pups went to Japan, and some American records suggest that at least two were used by the United States Navy.

*Formerly A6164, this Pup was interned in Holland in 1917 and was used by the Luchtvaart Afdeling as LA-41.*

**Type:** *Single-seat fighter.* **Power:** *One 80-h.p. Le Rhône 9C nine-cylinder rotary engine; one 80-h.p. Gnome or 80-h.p. Clerget, both seven cylinder rotary engines; one 100-h.p. Gnome Monosoupape nine-cylinder rotary engine.* **Armament:** *One fixed, synchronized 0.303-in. Vickers machine-gun; the Sopwith 9901 and 9901a had one 0.303-in. Lewis machine-gun and some had provision for eight Le Prieur rockets. Various attempts were made to fit a Lewis gun to Vickers-armed Pups.* **Performance:** *(Le Rhône): Maximum speed 111.5 m.p.h. at ground level, 105 m.p.h. at 5,000 ft., 102 m.p.h. at 10,000 ft.; climb to 5,000 ft., 5 min. 20 sec.; to 10,000 ft., 14 min.; service ceiling 17,000 ft.; endurance 3 hours. (Monosoupape) Maximum speed 110 m.p.h. at ground level, 107 m.p.h. at 6,500 ft., 104 m.p.h. at 10,000 ft.; climb to 6,500 ft., 7 min. 5 sec.; to 10,000 ft., 12 min. 25 sec.; service ceiling 18,500 ft.; endurance 1¾ hours.* **Weights:** *(Le Rhône): Empty 787 lb., loaded 1,225 lb.; (Monosoupape) empty 856 lb., loaded 1,297 lb.* **Dimensions:** *Span, 26 ft. 6 in.; length, 19 ft. 3¾ in.; height, 9 ft. 5 in.; wing area, 254 sq. ft.*

## SOPWITH TRIPLANE

At about the time when the prototype Pup first went to France, the first Sopwith triplane passed its final inspection at the Sopwith factory; the date was 28th May 1916. By that date, sufficient experience of air fighting had been gained for designers to understand that speed, manoeuvrability and the widest possible field of view for the pilot were essentials in a single-seat fighter. The radical step of adopting the triplane configuration had been taken in the hope that it would produce a highly manoeuvrable aircraft with a good outlook from the cockpit; the narrow chord (3 ft. 3 in.) of the mainplanes minimized the movement of the centre of pressure with changes in the angle of attack and permitted the use of a relatively short fuselage, thus enhancing manoeuvrability. The narrow wings obscured little of the pilot's field of view; the centre mainplane was level with his eyes.

In construction the triplane was remarkably conventional and simple. The fuselage was generally similar to that of the Pup but the disposition of spacers, formers and stringers differed; the engine was the 110-h.p. Clerget 9Z rotary, the diameter of which was 1020 mm.

*The prototype triplane, N500, at Chingford, with top centre section covered with transparent material.*

*Standard production triplane of No. 1 Squadron, R.N.A.S.*

whereas that of the Pup's 80-h.p. Le Rhône was 945 mm. The entire tail unit of the prototype, N500, and the first production triplanes was identical with that of the Pup but the incidence of the triplane's tailplane could be varied in flight by rotating a wheel mounted on the inboard side of the starboard centre-section strut within the cockpit.

Each wing panel had two main spars but these were so close together that single, broad-chord interplane and centre-section struts could be employed. A single landing wire and one pair of flying wires were fitted on either side; the top and bottom wings were braced as a biplane structure with the middle wing carried between the struts. All three wings had ailerons.

Harry Hawker, the Sopwith company's test pilot, had no qualms about the triplane's seemingly sketchy bracing, for he looped the prototype three minutes after its first take-off. At that time the triplane's centre section was covered with transparent material and no armament was fitted. A single Vickers gun was installed centrally immediately in front of the cockpit and, in mid-June 1916, the prototype triplane was sent to join the first Pup at the aerodrome of 'A' Squadron, R.N.A.S., Furnes. Less than a quarter of an hour after its arrival in France it was sent up to attack an enemy aircraft. The squadron diary recorded that the triplane could reach 12,000 ft. in 13 mins.

The general performance of the aircraft was very good, its climbing performance phenomenal. Like the Pup, it was ordered for both the R.N.A.S. and the R.F.C.; the naval triplanes were ordered from the Sopwith company; the initial War Office contract, allocated to Clayton and Shuttleworth, was for 166 triplanes to be numbered A9813–A9978.

The block A9000–A9099 was allocated for 100 triplanes to be built by the Sopwith company; it is possible that these too were intended for the R.F.C. The first Sopwith-built production triplane, N5420, was sent to Clayton and Shuttleworth as a pattern.

The second prototype, N504, which had a 130-h.p. Clerget engine, was flying by September 1916. On the 22nd of that month Squadron Commander Harry Busteed flew it at Hendon and found that its speed was 116 m.p.h. at ground level. It was again at Hendon in November 1916.

On 30th September 1916 Sir Douglas Haig wrote to the War Office, warning that British air superiority over the Somme was seriously threatened by the new German fighters and

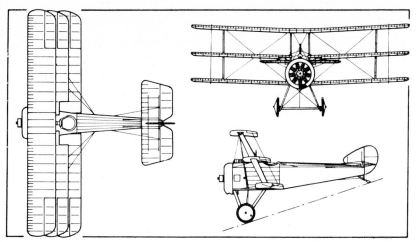

*Captured intact by the Germans, this triplane had the later smaller tailplane.*

urging "a very early increase in the numbers and efficiency of the fighting aeroplanes" at his disposal. The first consequence of this request was the formation of No. 8 Naval Squadron to work with the R.F.C. A further letter from Haig, written on 16th November 1916, asked for twenty extra fighting squadrons to be added to his earlier estimate of the needs for the spring of 1917. The Admiralty responded with substantial transfers of aircraft and engines to the R.F.C.; ultimately it was agreed in February 1917 that all Spads VII ordered for the R.N.A.S. would be exchanged for all the Sopwith triplanes ordered for the R.F.C.

*One of the two-gun triplanes built by Clayton & Shuttleworth.*

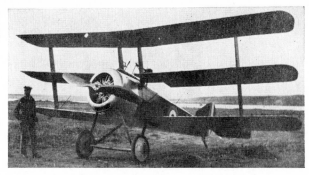

*A standard triplane with an unusual installation of a Lewis gun in addition to the normal single Vickers.*

For some reason as yet unexplained, this led to a substantial reduction in the number of triplanes ordered. In the event, only N5420–N5494 and N6290–N6309 were ordered from Sopwith, N533–N538 and N5350–N5389 from Clayton and Shuttleworth, and N5910–N5934 from Oakley Ltd. of Ilford. As mentioned above, N504 was the second prototype, with the 130-h.p. Clerget; N524 and N541–N543 were triplanes that were lent to the French government and later returned to the R.N.A.S. The six aircraft N533–N538 had twin Vickers guns. A few of these triplanes were used operationally, but the single gun remained the standard armament. At least one triplane was experimentally fitted with a Lewis gun, but it could not be used effectively.

As only three aircraft were delivered by Oakley Ltd., total production of the triplane cannot have exceeded 150. The production aircraft resembled N500, but had the upper centre section covered with fabric. The first prototype itself remained in operational use at Dunkerque until it was finally written off on 17th December 1917; the transparent covering of its centre section was replaced by ordinary fabric at an early stage and the aircraft survived several minor mishaps during its career.

The first production triplanes appeared late in 1916. By mid-February 1917, Naval squadrons Nos. 1 and 8 had been re-equipped with the new Sopwith, and Nos. 9, 10 and 12 also flew the type with distinction. 'B' Flight of No. 10 Naval Squadron, the redoubtable Black Flight led by Flight Commander Raymond Collishaw, scored many victories between May and July 1917; Collishaw himself destroyed seven enemy aircraft and drove down seventeen out of control during that period. The work of the Naval squadrons during the Battle of Arras earned the triplane a considerable reputation, so much so that the official historian came to write "The sight of a Sopwith Triplane formation, in particular, induced the enemy pilots to dive out of range."

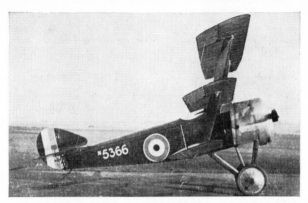

Most of the operational triplanes had the 130-h.p. Clerget and, from February 1917 onwards, a smaller tailplane and elevators were fitted as opportunity offered. The new surfaces had a span of 8 ft. and a total area of 23.6 sq. ft.; corresponding dimensions for the original surfaces were 10 ft. 1 in. and 34.8 sq. ft. On the later tailplanes the leading edge was shorter than the trailing edge. The new tailplane improved markedly the aircraft's response to the controls.

The smaller tailplane was the only significant change that was made to the triplane during its operational career and the aircraft seems to have had singularly few modifications, experimental or otherwise. In December 1916 N5423 was tested with wings of 3 ft. 6 in. chord. Its performance was better than that of the standard triplane, but production was not interfered with and the original wings were retained on all production aircraft. At a late stage, after the triplane's withdrawal from operations, the wing bracing was strengthened. In 1918 N5912, then on the strength of the School of Aerial Fighting at Marske, was flying with auxiliary mid-bay flying wires on its top wings; and on some aircraft a spanwise compression strut was fitted between the centre-section struts immediately above the gun to prevent bowing of the struts in aerobatics.

At least one aircraft was tested with a 110-h.p. Le Rhône engine at a loaded weight of 1,451 lb.; the empty weight was recorded as 1,095 lb. Performance was comparable with that provided by the Clerget; indeed the climbing performance was improved, 10,000 ft. being reached in 9 min. 20 sec. Speed at that height was 108.5 m.p.h.; at ground level it was 115.5 m.p.h. As there was no overall advantage in the use of the Le Rhône, the Clerget remained the standard engine.

The triplane's operational career was brief. As early as July 1917 it began to be replaced by the Camel in Naval squadrons Nos. 8 and 9, and by mid-October only No. 1 Naval still had triplanes. Many pilots were reluctant to give up their elegant and tractable mounts for the squat and wilful Camel.

Few triplanes saw service outside the European theatre of war. Early in 1917 N5431 was sent to No. 2 Wing, R.N.A.S., then operating from Mudros in the Aegean. It was extensively damaged at Salonika on 26th March 1917 while being flown by Flight Lieutenant J. W. Alcock, but was apparently rebuilt and was in action on 30th September 1917. Possibly some parts of the damaged components found their way into the single-seat fighter that Alcock built at Mudros in the summer of 1917 (see Vol. I, pages 6–8).

The triplanes N5385 and N5388 were presented to the French government. The Germans claimed to have shot down N5388 in September 1917 but did not state the name of its pilot, consequently it is not known whether the aircraft was in French service at that time.

On 4th May 1917 N5486 left the R.N.A.S. depot at the White City, destined for Russia. It was flown on the eastern front, and by the winter of 1917–18 it had been fitted with skis in place of its wheels. It may be the Sopwith

*Triplane N5912 photographed at Marske in 1918, with augmented wing bracing consisting of additional flying wires attached to the mid-bay points of both spars of the top wing.*

*Triplane with 110-h.p. Le Rhône engine.*

triplane that has been reported to exist still in Moscow.

A few Sopwith triplanes survived until the Armistice. Among these was N5430, which had been transferred to the R.F.C. It was at Orfordness for a time, and was fitted with an Aldis sight, an unusual refinement that the standard R.N.A.S. triplanes did not have. It was still in use in October 1918; on the 1st of that month it visited Farnborough, but returned to Orfordness, whence it had come on the same day. N5912 still exists, having been used for training purposes at Marske throughout 1918.

Few Allied aircraft made so great an impression on the enemy as did the Sopwith triplane; possibly only the Nieuport 11 scout could be compared with the triplane in this respect. That the enemy thought there must be some magic in the triplane configuration is

proved by the remarkable profusion of German and Austrian triplane fighters that were built in 1917 after the Sopwith had made its startling appearance in the skies of France.

*The only triplane to go to Russia, N5486, fitted with a ski undercarriage.*

**Type:** *Single-seat fighter.* **Power:** *One 110-h.p. Clerget 9Z, 130-h.p. Clerget 9B, or 110-h.p. Le Rhône nine-cylinder air-cooled rotary engine.* **Armament:** *One fixed, synchronized 0.303-in. Vickers machine-gun; a few triplanes had twin Vickers guns.* **Performance:** *(130-h.p. Clerget): Maximum speed 116 m.p.h. at 6,000 ft., 114 m.p.h. at 10,000 ft., 105 m.p.h. at 15,000 ft.; climb to 6,500 ft., 6 min. 20 sec., to 10,000 ft., 10 min. 35 sec., to 15,000 ft., 19 min.; service ceiling 20,000 ft.; endurance, 2¾ hours.* **Weights:** *(130-h.p. Clerget): Empty, 993 lb., loaded 1,415 lb.* **Dimensions:** *Span, 26 ft. 6 in.; length, 19 ft. 6 in.; height, 10 ft. 6 in.; wing area, 231 sq. ft.*

## SOPWITH L.R.T.Tr.

Like the Armstrong-Whitworth F.K.12 and Vickers F.B.11, the Sopwith three-seat triplane was intended to be a long-range escort fighter, and was powered by a 250-h.p. Rolls-Royce engine. The aircraft's long flight endurance and the emphasis placed on a good field of fire in all upward directions strongly suggest an alternative application in the anti-Zeppelin role. The Sopwith was apparently designed basically as a two-seater with pilot and observer in a conventional tandem arrangement; the provision of a small streamlined nacelle under the top centre section is hinted at in a Sopwith design drawing dated 13th March 1916, but its size and position suggest that it may have been intended to be no more

*The three-seat triplane under construction in the Sopwith works, 1916, with the top gunner's nacelle in its original form and position.*

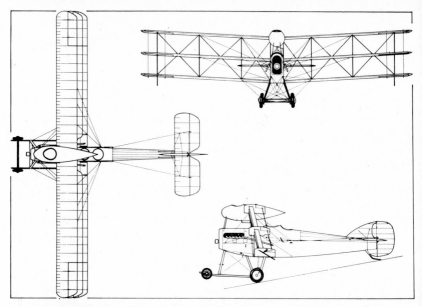

than a very large gravity tank.

In the Sopwith experimental shop the L.R.T.Tr. was contemporary with N500, the prototype Clerget triplane. The aircraft was built as a three-seater: a streamlined nacelle much larger than originally envisaged was built round the upper centre section, projecting forward as far as the reduction-gear casing of the engine. This nacelle was large enough to accommodate a gunner, who sat just ahead of the leading edge of the top wing.

The design of the top-wing nacelle was subsequently modified; it was set slightly farther back, the nose was shorter and blunter, and the under-floor part housed a gravity petrol tank. The pilot occupied the front cockpit in the fuselage, and there was dual control for the rear gunner, who had a single Lewis gun on a cranked pillar mounting.

Although the early design drawings depict the radiator behind the engine, the L.R.T.Tr. was in fact built with a large frontal radiator.

*The aircraft as completed, with modified nacelle.*

So deep was the top decking of the fuselage that the pilot sat wholly above the upper longerons. All the space under his cockpit right forward to the firewall was occupied by an enormous fuel tank. The undercarriage was basically a V-strut structure with the usual Sopwith divided axle. The exposed position of the top gunner demanded that the risk of overturning should be minimized, consequently substantial horizontal members carrying an additional pair of wheels projected ahead of the airscrew. The entire undercarriage assembly was clumsy and ugly, but it had the peculiar virtue that the aircraft could rest either tail-down or tail-high.

The mainplanes had a chord of only 4 ft.; their main spars were placed close enough together for plank-type interplane struts like those of the single-seat triplanes to be used. Ailerons were fitted to all wings, and the bottom mainplanes had at their inboard ends airbrake flaps similar to those of the 1½ Strutter. The tail unit was structurally conventional but the vertical surfaces were considerably larger than those originally designed.

The Sopwith L.R.T.Tr. looked clumsy and ponderous, and was probably a dangerous aeroplane. It was never put to the test of combat, presumably because the operational use of suitable machine-gun synchronizing mechanisms confirmed that fighting was best left to smaller and more agile aircraft. In the anti-Zeppelin field, too, several successes had been scored by more conventional aircraft. Whatever the reason for its demise, the big Sopwith three-seater was not developed; the fact that neither it nor either of its competitors was submitted for official tests suggests that a sudden change in official requirements was a probable reason.

**Type:** *Three-seat long-range fighter.* **Power:** *One 250-h.p. Rolls-Royce Mk. 1 (Eagle I) twelve-cylinder water-cooled engine.* **Armament:** *Two 0.303-in. Lewis machine-guns.* **Performance:** *No details available.* **Weights:** *No details available.* **Dimensions:** *Span, 52 ft. 9 in.; length, 35 ft. 3 in.*

## SOPWITH HISPANO-SUIZA TRIPLANE

Closely following the Clerget-powered triplane, a second Sopwith triplane fighter was designed and built in 1916. This was a completely different aeroplane that was designed round the new Hispano-Suiza engine, the celebrated V-8 designed by Marc Birkigt that,

*The first Hispano-Suiza triplane at Brooklands.*

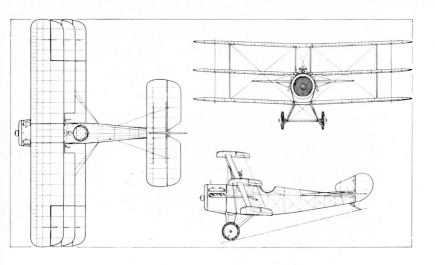

*The second aircraft, N510, which had a 200 Hispano-Suiza engine.*

*N510 with modified fuel system.*

to the 1½ Strutter; in particular its tail unit appeared to be identical with that of the two-seater. The configuration and dimensions of the Hispano-Suiza engine were known a full year before examples of the new power unit reached England, and it is not impossible that the Hispano-powered Sopwith triplane may have been an earlier design than the Clerget triplane but had to wait some time for its power unit.

Two aircraft, numbered N509 and N510, were built; the first had a 150-h.p. direct-drive Hispano-Suiza, the second a 200-h.p. geared engine. Apart from different cowling details and the higher thrust line and left-hand air-screw of N510, the two aircraft were almost identical. N510 had a different fuel system embodying a gravity tank in the top centre section. The only feature common to the Clerget and Hispano-Suiza triplanes was the interplane bracing: both had plank-type struts and the same seemingly sketchy arrangement of flying and landing wires.

Both N509 and N510 had a circular nose radiator, and the engine installation was generally similar to that of the later Sopwith T.1 and B.1. This suggests that it must have been found satisfactory on the triplane. The fuselage was deep, and for a single-seat fighter, capacious. Indeed, it may have been too capacious, for the pilot sat well down in the cockpit with his Vickers gun some inches above eye level. His view for landing and fighting must have been poor.

The mainplanes were larger in all dimensions than those of the Clerget triplane: the chord (4 ft. 3 in.) was a full foot greater, and the wing area was almost 50% more than that of the rotary-powered type. Ailerons were fitted to all three wings; their total area of 49 sq. ft. was 15 sq. ft. more than that of the Clerget triplane's surfaces.

Both Hispano-Suiza triplanes were flying in

in various forms and derivatives, was to power thousands of Allied aircraft before the Armistice was signed.

For this more powerful engine, of which a 200-h.p. version was in early prospect, a bigger aircraft than the Clerget triplane was designed. Whereas the rotary-powered aircraft had obviously close affinities with the Pup, the Hispano-Suiza triplane seemed to owe more

1916, but it is doubtful whether N510 saw 1917. It was reported to be at Eastchurch in December 1916, but it was destroyed during its trials. It may have been the Sopwith triplane of which Air Chief Marshal Sir Arthur Longmore wrote in his book *From Sea to Sky*:

"It was at Eastchurch that I saw, for the first and only time, the effect of 'tail flutter', which caused a fatal accident to the pilot of a new Sopwith triplane within a few feet of where I was standing. The pilot was doing a speed test low down, when I saw the tail flutter up and down twice before breaking away completely from the fuselage."

The 150-h.p. triplane N509 had a longer, though non-operational, career. It was flown at various R.N.A.S. aerodromes; like N510 it was tested at Eastchurch, and may have been used in attempts to determine the cause of N510's tail flutter, for Harry Busteed flew it on 2nd January 1917 and noted "tail vibrations" against the entry in his log book. In March 1917, N509 was at Westgate. By July it

was at Manston, where it was flown by Flight Sub-Lieutenant Lofft on the 7th of that month. Apparently it remained on Manston's charge, for it was written off there, after fair wear and tear, on 29th October 1917.

Official test reports on these aircraft have yet to be found, but the scanty figures that have survived suggest that, in speed and climb, performance was good. But the pilot's view was poor, manoeuvrability cannot have equalled that of the Clerget triplane, and Hispano-Suiza engines were in demand for the S.E.5a production programme. The Sopwith Hispano triplane could not, therefore, be considered for production.

**Type:** *Single-seat fighter.* **Power:** *One 150-h.p. or 200-h.p. Hispano-Suiza eight-cylinder water-cooled engine.* **Armament:** *One fixed, synchronized 0.303-in. Vickers machine-gun.* **Performance:** *Speed 120 m.p.h. Climb to 10,000 ft., 9 min.* **Weights:** *No details available.* **Dimensions:** *Span, 28 ft. 6 in.; length, 23 ft. 2 in.; wing area, 340 sq. ft.*

# SOPWITH F.1 CAMEL

Six months were to elapse after the appearance of the first Sopwith triplane until the next single-seat fighter emerged from the experimental shop of the Canbury Park Road works. The new type reverted to the biplane layout, doubtless because it had been found that, great though the advantages of the triplane configuration could be, it imposed limits on the speed that could be attained.

Designated Sopwith F.1, the new fighter was powered by a 110-h.p. Clerget 9Z rotary engine and was armed with two Vickers machine-guns firing through the disc swept by the airscrew. It was in its armament that the F.1 represented the greatest advance upon its predecessors, and offered British fighter pilots the

means of meeting the new Albatros single-seaters on equal terms. The guns were partially enclosed in a humped fairing that quickly earned the aircraft the nickname "Camel". This name was immediately popular and eventually had to be recognized officially.

The Camel bore a general family resemblance to the Pup but had a deeper fuselage in which the pilot sat well forward. The main masses of engine, fuel, armament and pilot were thus kept close together, an arrangement that enhanced manoeuvrability but placed the cockpit between the rear centre-section struts, from which position the pilot's view was somewhat restricted.

As originally conceived, the F.1 was to

*The first prototype Sopwith F.1, with 110-h.p. Clerget engine, one-piece top wing with no central cut-out, and sloping decking over gun breeches.*

*The Sopwith F.1/1, which had tapered wings and I-type interplane struts, at Brooklands.*

*This front view of the F.1/1 at Martlesham Heath shows that this aircraft had a central cut-out in the centre section to give the pilot some upward view.*

have equal dihedral on upper and lower wings, but it was thought that production would be facilitated if the top wing were made in one piece. The design was therefore revised; the top wing was made straight and the dihedral angle of the lower wings doubled in rough compensation. With a one-piece upper wing

the F.1 prototype was passed by the Sopwith experimental department on 22nd December 1916.

This was the first of several prototypes, some of which were built as private ventures. Two F.1s numbered N517 and N518 were ordered by the Admiralty; the first of these was tested at Brooklands on 26th February 1917; by May 1917 N518 was at Martlesham

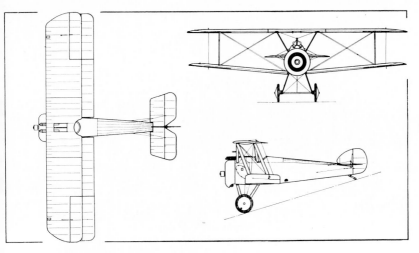

*Possibly the Sopwith F.1/2, this prototype retained the one-piece upper wing of the first prototype and the original short ailerons, but had a cut-out in the centre of the top wing.*

Heath, fitted with the first 150-h.p. A.R.1 engine.

The aircraft that was apparently regarded by the Sopwith company as the second prototype was designated F.1/1 and differed from the F.1 in having tapered wings with single broad-chord interplane struts. Powered by a 130-h.p. Clerget 9B engine, the F.1/1 did not undergo its official tests until May 1917. Its performance showed no improvement over that of the constant-chord F.1 and it was not developed.

*Possibly the F.1/3 modified to full production standard, this prototype had a three-piece upper wing and lengthened ailerons.*

*F.1 Camel with 150-h.p. Bentley B.R.1 engine and enlarged cut-outs in centre section. The aircraft is of No. 201 Squadron, R.A.F., and the additional openings in the engine cowling were made to provide additional cooling on the frequent ground-attack missions flown by the squadron during the summer of 1918.*

The F.1/1 had been preceded at Martlesham in March 1917 by the F.1/3 which was then powered by a 130-h.p. Clerget 9B. This aircraft still had the one-piece upper wing and short ailerons but, as on another prototype (which may have been the F.1/2), a cut-out was provided in the centre section in order to improve the pilot's upward view.

The F.1/3 was regarded as the production-type prototype. It was tested with alternative engines: the 110-h.p. Le Rhône 9J in May 1917, the 140-h.p. Clerget 9Bf in the following July. The production Camel differed from the F.1/3 in having its upper wing made in three parts; longer ailerons were also fitted.

First deliveries were of Camels for the R.N.A.S. from the Sopwith-built batch N6330–N6379, beginning on May 7th 1917. The R.N.A.S. Camels had either the 150-h.p. B.R.1

or the 130-h.p. Clerget; throughout the summer of 1917 the re-equipment of R.N.A.S. squadrons Nos. 3, 4, 6, 9 and 10 proceeded. The first War Office contract for Camels was given on 22nd May 1917 and was initially for 250 aircraft (B2301–B2350) to be built by Ruston Proctor & Co.; the 130-h.p. Clerget was specified. Further orders were placed in June 1917 with the Portholme Aerodrome (for B4601–B4650) and the Sopwith company (B3751–B3950). In the latter case the 110-h.p. Le Rhône and 130-h.p. Clerget were the specified engines but many of the Sopwith-built aircraft went to the R.N.A.S. and were fitted with the 150-h.p. B.R.1.

No. 70 Squadron was the first R.F.C. unit to have the Camel; its re-equipment was complete by the end of 1917. From then until the end of the war the Camel was used on almost every front by many units of the R.F.C., R.N.A.S., Australian Flying Corps, l'Aviation Militaire Belge, the Royal Hellenic Naval Air Service and the United States Air Service. Well over 5,000 F.1 Camels were built by nine contractors, and the type was still in production at the time of the Armistice.

Until the end, the Le Rhône, Clerget 9B and 9Bf and B.R.1 remained the standard power units, but other engines were fitted. Some Camels had the 100-h.p. Gnome Monosoupape; this combination was tested at Martlesham Heath in August 1917. The recorded performance was comparable with that of the 130-h.p. Clerget Camel, but little use seems to have been made of the Mono-soupape version.

A later type of Monosoupape engine was rated at 150 h.p. and was controlled in an unusual manner by a multi-position ignition switch that provided a throttling effect by progressively cutting out pairs of cylinders. At the minimum power setting only one cylinder fired. An engine of this type was first

*Major W. G. Barker, D.S.O., M.C., Officer Commanding No. 139 Squadron, in his Camel B6313 at Villaverla. He later modified this aircraft in several ways and painted additional white stripes on the rear fuselage.*

*Installation of a 100-h. p. Gnome Monosoupape engine in B3811*

tested in a Camel in December 1917 and at least two British Camels were fitted with it. Performance was good but the engine was not adopted for British use.

The Camel installation of the 150-h.p. Monosoupape was revived in 1918 when the U.S. Air Service bought a number of the engines and wanted them put in Camels. The conversion was undertaken by Boulton and Paul Ltd. and an American Monosoupape Camel was tested in October 1918. The Armistice stopped further development.

At a late stage a trial installation of a 170-

*F6456 was still in use at Farnborough in 1923, and had auxiliary mid-bay flying wires on the upper wings.*

after pitifully few hours of flying instruction. Nevertheless it became one of the supreme dog-fighting aircraft in the aerial armoury of the Allies.

Because it was so sensitive the Camel was the cause of many accidents at training units. A two-seat version was therefore evolved in 1918 for training purposes. It will be described in the volume dealing with training aircraft.

In spite of its extreme sensitivity the Camel was used as a night fighter in Home Defence squadrons. It was found that pilots were momentarily blinded by the flash of their

h.p. Le Rhône 9R was made in F6394, which was tested at Martlesham Heath in February 1919. An earlier installation of this power unit had been made in France in B3891, a Camel that had been transferred to the French government.

In its flying qualities the Camel was devastatingly different from its docile and tractable predecessors. In the right hands it was astonishingly manoeuvrable but it was remorseless and savagely unforgiving of the kind of mistakes that were made by too many of the ill-trained young men who were required to fly it

guns, and the use of explosive and incendiary ammunition in synchronized guns was regarded as dangerous. For these reasons a modified Camel was evolved. Its cockpit was moved aft and the Vickers guns were replaced by twin Lewis guns on a double Foster mounting above the centre section. Various arrangements of armament were fitted to individual aircraft. This night-fighter version of the Camel was, like the similarly modified 1½ Strutters described on page 120, nicknamed the Sopwith Comic.

The standard power unit of the Camel

(*Left*) Camel with 150-h.p. Gnome Monosoupape engine for the United States Air Service, at Martlesham Heath, October 1918.

(*Right*) In February 1919 F6394, fitted with a 170-h.p. Le Rhône 9R engine and an enlarged rudder, was also tested at Martlesham.

(*Left*) B9175 of No. 44 Squadron, a Home Defence Camel with 110-h.p. Le Rhône engine.

*One of the specially modified Camels used by Home Defence squadrons. The cockpit was moved aft, a head fairing was fitted, and twin Lewis guns above the centre section replaced the two Vickers guns of the standard Camel. This aircraft was also of No. 44 Squadron.*

night fighter was the 110-h.p. Le Rhône. The rearward position of the pilot dictated a revision of the fuel system, and a standard B.E.2e tank was fitted in front of the cockpit. This version of the Camel was still in service when the war ended.

F.1 Camels were used in experiments in flying fighter aircraft from lighters at sea, sharing the work with their near relation, the Sopwith 2F.1. In July 1918 ditching trials of Camels began; different types of hydrovane were tried and flotation gear was fitted. The aircraft concerned were B3878 and B6229.

In December 1918 the Isle of Grain had tested a Camel with an enlarged rudder of 6 sq. ft. (the standard surface was 4.9. sq. ft.);

this aircraft later had a rudder 6.4 sq. ft. in area and an enlarged fin of 3.5 sq. ft. (standard 3 sq. ft.). Farnborough also fitted Camels with enlarged tail controls for spinning experiments; B2312 and H7363 were being tested with Imber self-sealing petrol tanks at Farnborough in February 1920; and D1965 and F6456 were still in use there in April 1923, having seen much service in the R.A.E's work on the study of inverted flight.

Some F.1 Camels were used by the U.S. Navy and a few went to Canada after the war. In the R.A.F. the type was superseded by the Snipe and all its associations are with wartime combat, but a few saw post-Armistice fighting against the Bolsheviks in Russia and Poland until 1920.

**Type:** *Single-seat fighter.* **Power:** *110-h.p. Clerget 9Z, 130-h.p. Clerget 9B, 140-h.p. Clerget 9Bf, 110-h.p. Le Rhône, 100-h.p. Gnome Monosoupape, 150-h.p. Bentley B.R.1, 150-h.p. Gnome Monosoupape, 170-h.p. Le Rhône 9R: all were 9-cylinder rotary engines.* **Armament:** *Two fixed, synchronized 0.303-in. Vickers machine-guns on standard Camel; two 0.303-in. Lewis machine-guns on night-fighter version.* **Performance** (130-h.p. Clerget): *Maximum speed 104.5 m.p.h. at 10,000 ft., 97.5 m.p.h. at 15,000 ft; climb to 10,000 ft., 11 min. 45 sec.; to 15,000 ft. 23 min. 15 sec.; service ceiling 18,000 ft.* **Weights** (130-h.p. Clerget): *Empty 962 lb., loaded 1,482 lb.* **Dimensions:** *Span, 28 ft.; length (Clerget) 18 ft. 9 in.; height 8 ft. 6 in.; wing area 231 sq. ft.*

*A much-modified F.1 Camel on a lighter. The aircraft has a single Vickers gun in the port position and two Admiralty Top Plane mountings for Lewis guns on the centre section. The undercarriage is a jettisonable steel-tube structure.*

# SOPWITH 2F.1 CAMEL

An intriguing question relating to the British military aircraft of the 1914–18 war is why it apparently took so long to get the Sopwith 2F.1 into production. The aeroplane that was in effect the prototype 2F.1 had the official serial number N5 and was flying as early as March 1917, yet production 2F.1s did not begin to appear until the autumn of 1917. Moreover, the prototype had appeared hard on the heels of the report of a special committee of the Grand Fleet appointed by Admiral Beatty to consider and report on the Fleet's requirement of aircraft. This committee presented its report on 5th February 1917;

one of the more significant recommendations was that some light cruisers and other selected ships should be equipped with the means of carrying and launching Sopwith Pups. At such a time the Camel's greater power and better performance should have recommended it automatically as an early substitute for the Pup.

By early 1917, when the F.1 Camel had appeared, the Sopwith Baby seaplane had been in operational use for two years and, being little more than a slightly refined version of the Tabloid seaplane that had won the Schneider Trophy contest in April 1914,

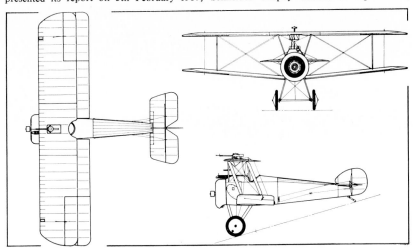

could not reasonably be expected to meet the more exacting operational demands of the immediate future. Presumably with a view to providing a more modern and better-armed aircraft as a replacement for the Baby, the Sopwith company designed a single-seat twin-float seaplane based on the Camel and intended for the 130-h.p. Clerget engine.

This seaplane was designated Sopwith FS.1 and was designed for shipboard use. Its main floats were plain pontoons, 11 ft. in length; the tail float was of circular cross section and fine streamline form. The aircraft was designed from the beginning to have a pair of jettisonable wheels for deck take-offs: this technique had been pioneered as early as 6th August 1915 by a Sopwith Schneider on H.M.S. *Campania*.

To conserve space on board ship the fuselage was made in two parts that were butt-jointed immediately behind the trailing edge of the lower wings and could be separated for stowage. The overall span was reduced to

27 ft. by fitting a centre section that was shorter than that of the F.1 Camel; the centre-section struts were of streamline-section steel tubing.

A significant change was made in the aircraft's armament. In place of the Camel's twin Vickers guns the FS.1 was intended to have a single Vickers gun in the port position and a fixed Lewis gun mounted inverted above the centre section, its ammunition drum fitting into the trailing edge cut-out. No doubt this was done in the hope that drums could be changed without the complication of a movable mounting to lower the gun.

Conclusive evidence of the existence of the FS.1 has yet to be found but it seems probable that it was built as N4 and that it was the "Camel seaplane" that was reported to have been wrecked late in March 1917.

The earliest known photograph of N5 shows it to be precisely a landplane version of the FS.1, even to the fitting of a fixed inverted Lewis gun on the centre section. It has been said that N5 crashed on its second flight on

*The prototype 2F.1 in its original form, still with the overwing Lewis gun mounted inverted on the centre section. The aircraft's serial number, N5, is clearly visible in this photograph.*

*N5 at a later date, fitted with tubes for eight Le Prieur rockets. At this time the aircraft was also equipped with a wireless set, the generator for which can be seen on the port side of the fuselage beside the cockpit.*

27th March 1917. If this did in fact occur, the damage must have been slight and quickly repaired, for Martlesham Heath's test report on the aircraft is dated March 1917, and on 4th April N5 was at the Isle of Grain. On that date it was flown by Harry Busteed, who wrote that he was "not very favourably impressed." The reference to a crash seems more likely to be a confusion with that of the FS.1 mentioned above.

By early June 1917 N5 had been fitted with launching tubes for eight Le Prieur rockets, four on each pair of interplane struts. Doubtless because it had proved to be well-nigh impossible to change drums on the inverted Lewis gun that weapon was now carried on an Admiralty Top Plane Mounting and could be let down through the central cut-out in the centre section for re-loading or upward firing. The Vickers gun was provided with 250 rounds

of ammunition and there were two 97-round drums for the Lewis; the eight rockets and their launching gear weighed 47 lb. A wireless set was also installed, and inflatable air bags in the fuselage provided a form of flotation gear. Thus loaded, N5 weighed 1,532 lb. in flying trim and climbed to 10,000 ft. in 11 minutes.

During the summer of 1917 much progress was made in deck flying, using Pups, including the evolution of the technique of flying from tiny platforms aboard warships. Despite the tricky flying characteristics of the F.1 Camel, the good performance of N5 must have made it seem to be a potentially good shipboard fighter. The whole of the foregoing history provides ample reasons why production of the type did not start until the summer of 1917. The situation is the more interesting because it is possible that N5 itself may have been intended to be a floatplane: the Sopwith

*Production 2F.1 Camel at the Isle of Grain, 5th November 1917.*

*Samson's 2F.1, N6623, on its lighter, 30th May 1918.*

*Culley's 2F.1, N6812, with twin Lewis guns above the centre section and quick-release catch on the undercarriage axle.*

company are reported to have made a second set of floats for a floatplane version of the Camel but there is no record of their use.

Fifty production aircraft (N6600–N6649) were ordered from Sopwith with the designation Sopwith 2F.1. Deliveries began in the autumn of 1917: N6603 was at the Isle of Grain on 5th November. The Sopwith company was then fully committed to production of Camels and Dolphins and to the development of further prototypes, consequently the initial order for fifty 2F.1s was supplemented by a contract for one hundred (N6750–N6849) from William Beardmore & Co. Ltd. of Dalmuir. The Beardmore company had been major contractors for the ship-board version of the Sopwith Pup and its derivative the Beardmore W.B.III. The last W.B.III (an S.B. 3D) was delivered in December 1917, and production of the Sopwith 2F.1 must have followed on immediately.

The Sopwith-built 2F.1 N6618 was at the Beardmore works on 4th February 1918 and was subsequently delivered to the R.N.A.S. at Rosyth. The first Beardmore-built 2F.1, N6750, flew on 20th February; it and N6751–N6754 were delivered to Rosyth. Of the others, it is known that N6755–N6773 were delivered to Turnhouse, and it seems that most of the others went initially to Renfrew. The last Beardmore-built 2F.1 of the first batch was delivered on 6th August 1918, and production continued with N7100–N7139, the last of these being delivered to Renfrew on 11th October. From the R.N.A.S. depots the 2F.1s were issued to capital ships but some went farther afield: for instance N6803 and N6808 went to Malta, N6812 and N6814 to Felixstowe.

The standard power unit of the production Sopwith 2F.1 was the 150-h.p. B.R.1, but the 130-h.p. Clerget was regarded as an alternative. The arrangement of the elevator and rudder control leads differed from that of the prototype: the pilot's control column was connected to a transverse rocking bar that bore external

*Modified 2F.1 Camel at Felixstowe with twin Vickers guns. This aircraft also had a jettisonable steel-tubing undercarriage similar to that of the modified F.1 illustrated on page 155. In the middle of the front row is Lt S. D. Culley.*

control levers for the elevator cables. It seems that a somewhat similar rudder control system was designed but abandoned in favour of direct cables. The dihedral angle of the lower wings was slightly increased to 5 deg. 30 min.

In June 1918 2F.1 Camels of the light cruisers *Sydney*, *Melbourne* and *Galatea* and of the carrier *Furious* were in action against German seaplanes. On 19th July seven 2F.1s of *H.M.S. Furious* bombed the Zeppelin base at Tondern with outstanding success; the Zeppelins L54 and L60 were destroyed in their sheds. Only two of the Camels returned to the naval task force that had brought them from Rosyth.

As another means of getting fast fighting

*A 2F.1 Camel fitted with airscrew guard and arrester-gear clips on the spreader bar takes off from H.M.S.* Eagle, *June 1920.*

aircraft to sea experiments were conducted with Sopwith F.1 and 2F.1 Camels carried on lighters that were towed by destroyers. The first test, on 30th May 1918, was a failure because the 2F.1's distinguished pilot, Lt.-Col. C. R. Samson, insisted on fitting his aircraft, N6623, with a skid undercarriage like that of the Sopwith 9901a Pup. The skids were supposed to run in troughs rigged up on the lighter, but in the event they jumped from their guides, fouled the supporting structure, and the Camel fell over the bows. Samson was, miraculously, unhurt.

Greater success was achieved by Lt. S. D. Culley who, flying the Beardmore-built N6812, made a successful take-off from a lighter towed by H.M.S. *Redoubt* on 10th August 1918 and shot down the Zeppelin L.53. This 2F.1 was armed with twin fixed Lewis guns on the centre section: reloading was not possible.

Culley and a Warrant Shipwright of Felixstowe had evolved a jettisonable undercarriage for the Sopwith 2F.1. This was demonstrated on 20th September 1918 by Lt. R. E. Keys, D.F.C., and a similar device was fitted to other F.1 and 2F.1 Camels.

Keys was the pilot of the other Beardmore-built 2F.1 that had been sent to Felixstowe, N6814, when it was successfully air-launched from the British airship R.23 in the summer of 1918. The Sopwith-built 2F.1 N6622 was also used in these experiments.

Of the 129 Sopwith 2F.1s that were on charge with the R.A.F. on 31st October 1918 all but 17 were with units of the Grand Fleet. Expanded production was envisaged, but the contracts given to the Fairey, Pegler and Sage companies were cancelled when the war ended.

Some 2F.1s saw continued operational use in the Baltic operations against the Bolsheviks in 1918–20. These were the aircraft of the carrier *Vindictive* and the light cruiser *Delhi*, which operated from the carrier and from a rough 300-yard landing strip at Koivisto. At least one 2F.1 had Esthonian markings, possibly at a later date, while retaining its British serial number. At the end of November 1919 three of *Vindictive*'s 2F.1 Camels were sent to Riga for the use of the Latvian forces; all three were still in use in August 1921.

The 2F.1 remained in British service as a

*One of H.M.S. Vindictive's 2F.1 Camels wearing Esthonian markings at the rough airfield at Koivisto, 1919.*

*The airship and overhead-wire landing gear fitted to the 2F.1 Camel N7352, 7th February 1921. This incorporated an airscrew guard and liberal bracing; the entire centre section was stripped of fabric to give the pilot the best possible upward view.*

carrier-borne fighter for some years after the war. At the Isle of Grain 2F.1s and Pups were flown in tests of overhead landing gear, the object of which was to enable aircraft to be retrieved by flying on to a cable carried outboard of a ship, stretched between two booms. This was clearly an extension of the wartime practice of flying fighters from battleships and was intended to avoid the otherwise inevitable loss of the aircraft after a flight at sea. A Camel, probably a 2F.1, was in use at Grain in March 1920, testing the device. Several different types of overwing hook were tested on a long cable stretched between tall posts, and by February 1921 N7352 had been fitted with an elaborate arrangement described as "airship and overhead wire landing gear for small craft". Thus Britain's R.A.F. anticipated by several years the U.S. Navy's work with airship-borne fighters; but the British idea was never developed.

In the post-war years some 2F.1s went to Canada and saw long service.

**Type:** *Single-seat shipboard fighter.* **Power:** *One 150-h.p. Bentley B.R.1 or 130-h.p. Clerget 9B nine-cylinder rotary engine.* **Armament:** *One fixed, synchronized 0.303-in. Vickers machine-gun; one 0.303-in. Lewis machine-gun on Admiralty Top Plane Mounting.* **Performance** *(B.R.1): Maximum speed 122 m.p.h. at 10,000 ft., 117 m.p.h. at 15,000 ft; climb to 10,000 ft., 11 min. 30 sec.; to 15,000 ft., 25 min.; service ceiling 17,300 ft.* **Weights** *(B.R.1): Empty 1,036 lb., loaded 1,530 lb.* **Dimensions:** *Span, 26 ft. 11 in.; length (B.R.1) 18 ft. 8 in.; height 9 ft. 1 in.; wing area 221 sq. ft.*

*Another view of the airship and overhead-wire landing gear.*

# ACKNOWLEDGEMENTS

Grateful acknowledgement is made to the following individuals and organizations from whom were obtained the illustrations on the pages listed hereunder. Other illustrations came from the author's collection. (t=top, m=middle, b=bottom of page)

*Aeromodeller:* 124, 150(b)
*Squadron Leader D. G. Beeton, R.A.F.:* 43.
*J. H. Blake:* 19.
*P. M. Bowers:* 120.
*C. J. Chabot:* 18(b).
*E. F. Cheesman:* 119(b), 138(t).
*Crown Copyright:* 17(b), 18(t), 21, 29(b), 31(b), 37, 42, 53, 54, 55, 59, 61, 62, 64, 66, 68, 69, 72, 74, 79, 80(t), 88(b), 89, 91, 93, 151.
*Ministry of Defence:* 17(t), 41, 94.
*'The Eye', R.A.F. Wyton:* 44.
*Flight International:* 101, 103(t), 137.
*F. Gerdessen:* 130(b).
*Hawker-Siddeley Aviation Ltd.:* 97, 106, 143.
*Imperial War Museum:* 16, 31(t), 33, 34, 40(b), 57, 71, 76, 78(t), 81(t), 88(t), 99, 129, 134(b), 142, 146(t), 148(b), 152(m), 159(t), 161(b).
*Egon Krueger:* 38, 40(t), 86(t).
*K. M. Molson:* 24, 115, 117(t).
*Harald Penrose, O.B.E., F.R.Ae.S.:* 118.
*Robey & Co. Ltd.:* 6, 8, 10, 110.
*Royal Aeronautical Society collection:* 25, 26, 29(t), 78(b), 82, 84, 87, 113
*R. C. Shelley:* 150(t).
*F. Yeoman:* 134(t), 138(b).

# INDEX